The Changing World of Atheism

The CHANGING WORLD *of* ATHEISM

Coming to Grips with Recent Atheist Strategies and Signs Pointing to God

Paul Chamberlain

CASCADE *Books* · Eugene, Oregon

THE CHANGING WORLD OF ATHEISM
Coming to Grips with Recent Atheist Strategies and Signs Pointing to God

Cascade Books
An Imprint of Wipf and Stock Publishers
199 W. 8th Ave., Suite 3
Eugene, OR 97401

www.wipfandstock.com

PAPERBACK ISBN: 979-8-3852-1883-7
HARDCOVER ISBN: 979-8-3852-1884-4
EBOOK ISBN: 979-8-3852-1885-1

Cataloguing-in-Publication data:

Names: Chamberlain, Paul [author].

Title: The changing world of atheism : coming to grips with recent atheist strategies and signs pointing to God / by Paul Chamberlain.

Description: Eugene, OR: Cascade Books, 2026 | Includes bibliographical references.

Identifiers: ISBN 979-8-3852-1883-7 (paperback) | ISBN 979-8-3852-1884-4 (hardcover) | ISBN 979-8-3852-1885-1 (ebook)

Subjects: LCSH: Atheism. | Apologetics. | Christianity and atheism. | Religion—Philosophy. | Faith and reason.

Classification: BL2747.3 C436 2026 (print) | BL2747.3 (ebook)

To Cadence Grace, Sophia Joy, and Ava Hope: three bright lights in a world that needs more grace, joy, and hope

The existence of God is not subjective. He either exists or he doesn't. You can have your own opinions but you can't have your own facts.
—Ricky Gervais

I do not feel obliged to believe that the same God who endowed us with sense, reason, and intellect had intended for us to forgo their use.
—Galileo

Contents

Introduction

THE AUDITORIUM WAS FILLED with atheists from around North America and even a few from further away. There were also others in attendance but not many since this was an atheist convention. A colleague and I had been invited to participate in a debate with two of their representatives as the opening act of the convention.

As the debate progressed, I listened closely to the case being made by our debate opponents. We had done this before but something was different today. The viewpoint being advocated was the same . . . or was it? The more I listened to the key concepts under discussion, the harder it was to tell. It was still atheism, at least they said it was, but both the packaging of this view and the way it was being supported were different.

The arguments I had expected, and prepared for, were hardly mentioned, but other things were. Even the very understanding of atheism itself seemed different, and tracking it all was a bit like trying to nail jelly to a wall. I quickly realized that new approaches were being developed by these atheist representatives, and, given how well connected they were within the atheist community throughout North America and beyond, this would not be an isolated event. The case for atheism was changing.

When it came time for rebuttal and cross examination, my colleague and I looked at each other and scrapped a good deal of what we had prepared. And, yes, we had studied these very debaters in our preparation. In those few minutes, we hastily developed some new approaches of our own built around what we were hearing from our atheist friends.

This debate turned out to be one of the most collegial and productive events I had ever been involved in. It marked the beginning of a journey of tracking a number of new and creative strategies atheists are using to argue their case. While some of them are extensions or revisions of older approaches, in a few cases genuinely new strategies are being employed. I first introduced some of these approaches to my students, then presented them at an academic conference where I received helpful feedback. This led to numerous discussions about them with interested colleagues, friends, and other audiences, and now this book represents an extended development of them.

The case for atheism is being advanced vigorously today in a flurry of recent books. Some of them are popular reads intended for a wide cross section of our culture with titles like *God? No! Signs You May Already Be An Atheist and Other Magical Tales*[1] (a humorous reinterpretation of the Ten Commandments) and *Why There Is No God: Simple Responses to Twenty Common Arguments for the Existence of God.*[2] Others are aimed at a more academic audience and have titles like *Atheism: The Case Against God*[3] and *The Oxford Handbook of Atheism.*[4] These are just a few of the recent books making the case in one way or another for the position that God does not exist. As Stephen Bullivant and Michael Ruse, the editors of *The Oxford Handbook to Atheism*, note, "The past several years have witnessed a remarkable growth in studies of atheism and related topics."[5]

As noted above, however, atheism is being portrayed and presented differently today, sometimes in ways that are confusing for Christians who attempt to engage their atheist friends. If you have engaged proponents of atheism recently, you will have experienced changes in the way they present their view. Such changes are even more likely if the proponents are well informed and connected

1. Jillette, *God? No!*
2. Navabi, *Why There Is No God.*
3. Smith, *Atheism.*
4. Bullivant and Ruse, *Oxford Handbook of Atheism.*
5. Bullivant and Ruse, *Oxford Handbook of Atheism*, 18.

to one of the growing number of atheist or skeptic associations throughout the world.

Who would have thought a viewpoint as seemingly straightforward and long-standing as atheism could undergo change in both its packaging and presentation? Unless we are tracking with these changes, however, we are in danger of being caught off guard when engaging our atheist friends. The "old" ways of reasoning with atheists may well fall flat in the face of more recent ways of both interpreting and presenting atheism.

In one sense, changes in the way atheists portray and argue their viewpoint are not surprising. Having encountered hard-hitting arguments from theist philosophers and others over the past few decades, atheists have naturally adjusted their approaches and strategies, like adherents of any viewpoint which is critiqued and challenged.

Three comments can be made about these changing strategies right off the top. First, while they may appear subtle or small at first glance, in some cases they are profoundly significant since they are connected to the very definition of atheism itself.

Second, these changing strategies can cause confusion, frustration, and even discouragement in those attempting to engage their atheist friends. Tracking them can sometimes feel like chasing smoke. When atheism is defined differently, and the case for it changes along with the definition, it can lead us to throw up our hands and wonder what just happened at the end of a conversation. What happened to the atheism I thought I knew? The label is the same, but everything else seems different.

This leads to the third comment which is that understanding these changing strategies is the key to having profitable conversations with people, and that really matters. It means we will be prepared to both ask and receive probing questions as we interact with our atheist friends. It also puts us in the enviable position of being able to learn more about other people's views and their reasons for holding them.

I have written this book with three purposes in mind. The first is to equip readers who wish to engage atheists or others in a helpful manner. To do this effectively, we need to be up-to-date, and this book is intended to be one modest step in that direction. To that end we will analyze a number of new ways in which atheists are both interpreting atheism and making the case for it. Understanding must come first, and this will be a primary focus of the first part of this book.

Secondly, we will assess and provide thoughtful responses to these atheist strategies. This will involve evaluating them to see where they succeed and where they do not. Our question will always be whether they provide an adequate case for atheism as their proponents claim. At times, this process may seem like philosophical hairsplitting, but the ideas we will dissect are critically important to the atheist proponents asserting them and, for that reason, must be important to anyone else wanting to evaluate them.

My third purpose in writing goes beyond theism, the belief in God, and is directed towards people who wonder whether the story of Christianity is true and worthy of our belief. As a young person full of questions myself, I could have used a resource which addressed them. Instead, I was advised to ask God to simply remove them. Needless to say, that is an interesting assignment for someone who is wondering whether there is a God in the first place. In the end, I did finally encounter one person and a group of authors who tackled the questions I had, and I will never forget the huge sigh of relief my struggling faith breathed just from the opportunity to read about and openly discuss them.

Christianity's most foundational claim is that there is a God who stands behind everything else that exists, including you and me. We should remind ourselves from time to time of how important this claim is for the rest of Christianity and of the ripple effect it would cause if discredited. If there is no God, then there is nothing left of the Christian story. There is no Son of God, no word of God, no acts of God, no forgiveness by God, no justice or love of God, no God who revealed himself in the person of Jesus, and it certainly makes no sense to pray to God. In fact, some Christian theologians and philosophers go as far as to define Christianity in its most basic form as consisting of two great convictions: first, there is a God; and second, this God has revealed himself in the person of Jesus of Nazareth.[6] Embrace those two big ideas and you are firmly on the Christian side. It is no wonder, then, that many of Christianity's strongest critics continue to focus their energies on this one teaching, namely, the existence of God. It is the most efficient attack imaginable. If it succeeds, then the rest of Christianity crumbles with it.

With this in mind, after evaluating a number of recent strategies employed by atheists to argue for their view, part 2 of this book will put forward a number of signs which point to the existence of God. A working knowledge of these signs will enhance our discussions with people who question the existence of God.

We can all grow in our ability to carry on constructive conversations, even about questions as foundational as this one, and the better we can do this, the more help we will be to those who question.

6. Plantinga, *Warranted Christian Belief*, 3. Plantinga goes on to add that Christians also believe that Jesus came to redeem us and that we are able to talk to him and about him.

PART 1

Exploring Atheist Strategies

Chapter 1

The Power of a Good Conversation

A FRIEND OF MINE was riding a bus one day and struck up a conversation with the man seated next to him. Both were interested in the other's work and life, and it soon came out that my friend believed in God. "Well, I don't," replied the man confidently. "I just couldn't."

After chatting with the man for a few minutes and inviting him to tell him more, my friend responded, "I take it then that you're an atheist."

"Yes, absolutely!" he said.

My friend was quiet for a moment and then decided to ask him the following question: "Do you really believe you could prove there is no God anywhere in or out of the universe?"

The man's reply was interesting and thoughtful. "Well, when you put it like that, I'm not sure I could prove the point either way. I guess there could be a God, but I haven't seen anything to convince me."

After a moment, my friend replied, "If you don't mind me saying so, you sound more like an agnostic than an atheist. You seem open to the possibility that God exists but don't feel you have enough information to say. Could that be true?"

The man thought for a moment and agreed. "Yes, I suppose that's probably what I am." From an atheist to an agnostic in five minutes.

Obviously, not all conversations go that quickly or smoothly, but we could take some lessons from my friend. His interest in the other person's life along with his inviting manner obviously worked to encourage openness on one of the issues from which we are all told to stay away—religion. That, in itself, is a worthwhile accomplishment. It helped that both he and his conversation partner were confident enough to freely share their views.

Furthermore, this conversation shows the power of asking a good question at the opportune moment. A well-thought-out question can shine a spotlight on ambiguities or assumptions made in conversation. It can focus discussion where it needs to be. Asking good questions concerning theism and atheism today, however, requires some understanding of the new and creative ways some atheists are defining and arguing for their position. We will be exploring a number of them in this book.

We should not overlook how important this man's change from atheism to agnosticism was. It was not a trivial transition even though, in his case, it happened quite quickly. Atheism is significantly different from agnosticism since each position has different implications for how hard a person will investigate the matter. If we think our lost wallet or glasses *just might* be somewhere in the kitchen, then it will make sense for us to look for these items there. If, however, we already know, or are convinced, that they are not there, we won't spend any time looking for them in that room. Why waste our time? We already "know" they're not there.

That is the difference between the atheist and agnostic outlooks. Agnosticism, by definition, is open to the possibility that God might exist. The agnostic just doesn't know, and unless he thinks this information is beyond human reach, it will make sense to consider the matter further. Not so for atheists. If they are true to their atheism, they will spend little time on the question. They "know" God is not out there, so there is no need to investigate the matter further. It matters whether one is a self-described atheist or agnostic. In the next chapter, we'll see how a conversation between people who hold these different positions might play out.

Chapter 2

Three Kinds of People

My father had a dry sense of humor. His ability to get people to laugh at his jokes always intrigued me because when I tried the same jokes, they usually elicited more of a head shake than a laugh. Here is an example: "There are three kinds of people in this world—those who can count and those who cannot." That's it, the whole joke right there. If you're thinking it doesn't sound very funny, I agree, at least not on paper. But when he told it, people laughed. It had to be something in the delivery. We always felt like telling people, "Don't encourage him, he has more."

One other thing my father and mother passed on to me was a positive view of Christianity. They both modelled their faith consistently, and our home was a happy one. My growing-up years included many family vacations, fun times, sporting activities, plenty of ice cream, and a consistent commitment to Christian truth claims. But as I got older, a serious question entered my mind: How did I know this whole belief system about God, Jesus, salvation, forgiveness of sins, and the rest was true? Or even credible? I knew we believed it, but I also knew that did not make something true. My big question was how one is to proceed with questions like this. For me it became a journey of asking questions, talking with others, reading good books, thinking hard, and even praying, although at times I wasn't sure anyone was there to hear my prayers. It was all part of my questioning. I finally decided, if God was there, he would hear them. If not, no harm done.

When I began investigating the matter further, I came to see there were indeed three kinds of people when it came to the question of God's existence or, should I say, three major viewpoints on this question: theism, atheism, and agnosticism. Bertrand Russell, one of the most influential atheists of the twentieth century, set out a concise, standard traditional definition of one of the viewpoints—atheism—in his 1957 book *Why I Am Not a Christian*. In doing so, he also contrasted it with the other two positions in this way:

> An atheist, like a Christian, holds that we can know whether or not there is a God. The Christian holds that we can know there is a God, the atheist, that we can know there is not. The agnostic suspends judgment, saying that there are not sufficient grounds either for affirmation or for denial.[1]

It is a simple and clear definition. It affirms that both atheists and theists claim to know something significant about the universe. Moreover, both believe their truth claims are true, and, as such, these two views stand in stark contrast with one another. The only position not claiming to know something is agnosticism. As Russell rightly put it, agnostics suspend judgment on the question of God's existence.[2]

We can go further than Russell's definition, however, because there are actually two types of agnosticism, and we need to distinguish between them. The first type, sometimes called skepticism, is simply the stance that says, "I do not know whether God exists or not." It is nothing more than a statement of one's own lack of information on this question. The other kind, sometimes referred to as hard agnosticism, makes a stronger claim and declares that *we cannot know* whether such a being as God exists. This includes all of us regardless of how smart we are or how much we have

1. Russell, *Basic Writings*, 557–58.
2. Russell, *Basic Writings*, 557–58.

researched the matter. It is beyond our capacity as finite human beings to know the answer to such a profound question as this one. As we'll see going forward, the difference between these two types of agnosticism is real, and we will need to treat them differently.

Consider the way three university students wrestle with how to articulate their various views on the existence of God. Their names are Emmanuel, Zach, and Claire, and they are having lunch after their first philosophy of religion class.

EMMANUEL. (*Opening his lunch bag and letting out a sigh.*) Well, thank God for respite!

ZACH. Thank God? It sounds like you've got the question about God figured out already.

EMMANUEL. Oh I have plenty of questions, but I do believe there is a God.

ZACH. So you're a theist.

EMMANUEL. From the sounds of things, you're not.

ZACH. How do you figure that?

EMMANUEL. Just a hunch. You called me a theist, and it didn't sound like you were including yourself in that group.

ZACH. You're right. I'm an atheist. I'm happy leaving religion to others. It's called freedom of religion.

CLAIRE. (*Leaning forward to interject.*) It sounds more like freedom *from* religion, in your case.

ZACH. That too. In this country we can choose to believe in God or any religion we want, or none at all. That's my choice. I'm a "none."

CLAIRE. (*Chuckling.*) It sounds like Emmanuel is not the only one who has the issue all figured out. Listen to you both. You're making it sound like there are only two choices here. Emmanuel, you believe there is a God. Zach, you don't. But I don't believe either of your views.

Zach. Well, either there is a God or there is not. What are we missing?

Claire. I don't believe there is a God but . . .

Zach. So you're an atheist. Welcome to the club.

Claire. Not so fast. I also don't believe there is not a God.

Zach. Whoa! So you're just not saying.

Claire. Oh, I'm saying. I'm saying I don't have enough information on a question this big to commit to one view or the other. That's my position. I'm suspending judgment on the question.

Emmanuel. That sounds more like a non-position to me.

Claire. It's a position alright, a viewpoint. It has a name and everything. It's called agnosticism, and frankly, I'm not sure either of you have enough information to take the firm positions you're taking on this question.

Claire, Emmanuel, and Zach have articulated three views, and Russell's definition makes clear that each is an answer to a very important question about our universe: Is there a God behind it? Theists answer yes, atheists no, while agnostics say we either do not or cannot know. It's time to examine the various strategies employed by atheists in making the case for their position.

Chapter 3

Strategy #1: Shifting the Burden of Proof

MANY OF US PROBABLY assume that discussions of the existence of God will revolve around arguments and evidence, but that is not the way conversations will necessarily go anymore. In fact, there may be little interest in discussing arguments or evidence at all. The discussion may well shift to the question of who has to prove what in order to make their case.

Technically, this is known as the question of the burden of proof. While this may sound like a rather trifling or technical difference, it can take the discussion into an entirely new direction, one which can be disorienting if we're not prepared.

In the debate mentioned earlier in this book, after presenting a few arguments for theism and raising some challenges to atheism, we, the theists, called upon the atheist debaters to present reasons for their position. Since you're recommending atheism, we said, tell us why someone should think it is true. Our plan was to hear them out and then reply to their arguments in our next speeches. This had been my normal practice when engaging people with other perspectives, and it seemed like a natural question in this setting. We were expecting to hear about evil and suffering or the incoherence of talk about God or even the evils of religion, and we had come prepared to respond to these and a few others.

Instead of giving these or any other reasons to believe atheism, however, the atheist debaters cheerfully announced that neither they nor anyone else could prove it to be true. So they had no intention of presenting arguments at all.

It might sound like they were throwing up their hands and admitting defeat, but they were not. They went on to argue that this did not mean their position was flimsy or inadequate. Atheists, they said, have no obligation to provide reasons for their view. That job rests completely on theists. It is up to theists to show God exists. Atheists simply need to tell others why they do not find the arguments for theism persuasive. Once we have done that, they affirmed, we have made all the case we need to make for atheism.

To make matters more interesting, they went on to redefine atheism in a way that, at first, seemed like an insignificant technicality but, for their strategy, turned out to be a game-changer. We'll get to this new portrayal of atheism a bit later, but for now, it is sufficient to say that our responses took a different turn that evening.

Notice how this way of portraying and advocating atheism comes through in the conversation between our three philosophy students the next day as they wait in the classroom for the professor to arrive.

Zach. (*Turning to Claire.*) So you really think Emmanuel and I lack sufficient information to be either a theist or atheist? Is that what you said yesterday?

Claire. Exactly! Have you actually thought about how much you would need to know to answer a question like this one? Frankly, the confidence you both seem to have is a little over the top, don't you think?

Zach. Well I don't need more information to know why I'm an atheist.

Claire. You *are* pretty sure of yourself, aren't you. Do you really think you could prove there is no God?

Zach. Oh, that's a good one, Claire!

Claire. A good one?

ZACH. Yes. You've got the shoe on the wrong foot. I'm not the one with something to prove here.

EMMANUEL. (*Perking up.*) Just so I get this straight, Zach, are you saying you can't prove atheism, and yet you still believe it?

ZACH. Well, I didn't quite say that. What I said is I don't have to. You're the one with something to prove because you're telling us there is a God.

EMMANUEL. If I have to prove my position, why exactly don't you have to prove yours?

ZACH. Because the burden of proof is always on the person making the positive statement.

EMMANUEL. Ah yes, it's never on the one making the negative claim. Is that your position?

ZACH. I couldn't have said it better.

EMMANUEL. Well, there are arguments for God's existence out there.

ZACH. Yes, I remember hearing about some of them in a lecture I was invited to last year. As I remember, I didn't find them overly convincing.

CLAIRE. Can you see now why some of us take my position? You both should listen to yourselves for a minute. Emmanuel, you believe there is a God. Zach, you don't, and you say Emmanuel's arguments are unconvincing. But when he asks you for arguments for atheism, you don't have any. In fact, you don't even think you need any.

ZACH. So you think the best position is your non-position?

CLAIRE. Yes, I do, but it's not a non-position. As I said, it just means we admit up front that we do not have enough information to know whether God exists. Some agnostics go further and believe no one *could* know. After listening to you two, I can see why.

Emmanuel. That's harsh! I still say that one way to find out would be to hear the case for both theism and atheism. Then we could compare to see who makes the stronger case.

Zach. Still don't get it, do you, Emmanuel? Atheists have no need to make a case for our view. We're not the ones making the claim. That's your job since you're the one making the claim that God exists.

Emmanuel. (*Head shaking.*) Nice, convenient position you've worked out for yourself, Zach.

Zach. It's not me working anything out. It's the nature of atheism.

Claire. Hey guys, class is starting; we'll have to pick this up later.

The upshot of this is that we have three viewpoints on an important question with plenty of intelligent people holding each. Where do we go from here? We need to carefully consider this unusual way of defending atheism because it is part of a larger set of strategies which atheists are employing. Later in this book, we'll see that the debate over the burden of proof is a dynamic one and continues to take new turns, some of which involve intricate distinctions of which we should be aware. Some, like our atheist colleagues in the debate, go so far as to alter the very definition of atheism.

Figuring out these new strategies and responding to them will be a major part of this book, but before we get there, let's unpack further the concept of burden of proof and see how it has often functioned in the past. Then we'll turn to some of the new and creative ways it is being used today.

Chapter 4

What's So Important About the Burden of Proof?

THE ISSUE OF THE burden of proof arises when there is more than one viewpoint on a question. This is almost always the case with important questions whether political, ethical, scientific, philosophical, religious, or any other field of inquiry, and it certainly is the case with our question—"Is there a God?"

There are really two questions involved in the discussion of burden of proof:

1. Which of the opposing views on any question needs to be proven if the proponents are to successfully defend their views? Is it one or the other or both?
2. Is one of the views the default position such that it doesn't need to be proven or argued but rather is the one we can fall back to in the absence of overwhelming arguments for an opposing view?

The way we answer these two questions will have great effect upon how the discussion of any question goes and on what we conclude. Consider our normal procedure when facing a tough question, whether it be about animal rights, tax policy, or even where our next vacation should take place. We seek out the best reasons for the various options and evaluate them the best we can. When this involves discussion, we ask others why they hold their views and what problems they find with yours. Then we present reasons of our own, at least if we hope our view will be regarded as credible.

When inquiring into a question as important as God's existence, one which has deep implications for so many other areas of thought (the nature of our universe, humans, morality, the afterlife, etc.), it is natural to assume we would follow a similar procedure, and historically we have. Theistic philosophers have developed arguments involving the existence of the universe, of minds within it, of the orderliness seen in it, of moral values in people's minds, of Jesus of Nazareth, and even the existence of such entities as numbers. Atheists have replied to these and also developed arguments of their own. Each person in the discussion aims to show their view is the stronger one, and they do this by showing that the reasons for their view are superior to those for the opposite one. It all hinges on the strength of the reasons.

This is where things have taken a different and unexpected turn. Many atheists today, including the atheist debaters mentioned above, see no need to defend their view or present reasons for it. Rather, they regard atheism as the default position in the question of God's existence. All they need to do is find the arguments for theism unconvincing, and they are on good grounds accepting atheism.

This way of supporting atheism has become increasingly common in our times. Here is how the late Christopher Hitchens, well-known representative of new atheism, argued he had no duty to make a case for his position in a debate with Christian philosopher William Lane Craig:

> The proposition that atheism is true is a misstatement of what I have to prove and what we believe. . . . I don't have a special name for my unbelief in toothfairies or witches or Santa Claus. I just don't think that they're there. I don't have to prove a-toothfairyism . . . or a-witchism . . . or a-Santa Clausism. It's just that I think those who do believe in such things have never been able to make a plausible case for doing so. . . . Am I an atheist? Yes, . . . I've never been shown any evidence that any process

> observable to us cannot be explained by more satisfactory and more convincing means.[1]

When pressed by Craig as to whether he had any arguments which would lead to the conclusion that God does not exist, Hitchens repeated that his basis for atheism was simply that he found all arguments *for* the existence of God to be "fallacious or unconvincing."[2] Atheism was regarded as the default position, the one we can fall back to, and thus, there was no need to provide reasons for it. Clearly, a view that is elevated to the status of the default position enjoys great advantages.

Emmanuel discovered this in the dialogue in the previous chapter. When he offered to bring arguments for theism, and stated his willingness to hear opposing arguments from Zach, he was quickly rebuffed. Zach, the atheist, claimed he had no obligation to provide reasons for his position. That job rested on Emmanuel alone because, as Zach put it, he was the one making a claim here, namely, that God exists. This is a common assertion by atheists who make it to justify shifting the burden of proof to theism, and we will assess it later. For now, the point is that atheists who reason this way believe they have no need to present reasons in support of atheism.

I do not see this as happening by accident. In recent decades, theist philosophers have developed sophisticated responses to many atheistic arguments (unintelligibility of God-talk, problem of evil, etc.), and this has changed the debate. The result is that many atheists have conceded that their position—that God does not exist—cannot be proven but then have changed their argumentative strategy to claim that this is okay since they are not the ones with anything to prove in the first place.

This strategy has been employed passionately by a few well-known thinkers including Richard Dawkins, a British biologist and one of the world's most prominent atheists, and Canadian philosopher Dale Beyerstein. Both are atheists who have argued

1. The Hitchens–Craig debate referred to here can be found in Biola University, "Does God Exist?," 1:06.

2. Biola University, "Does God Exist?," 1:08, 1:20.

that the burden of proof should be placed squarely onto theism. We should note, however, that these thinkers have utilized this strategy as merely one alongside others. For Zach, in the dialogue above, and for many others like him, this strategy, when joined to a new definition of atheism which we will look at shortly, undercuts the need for any arguments at all. It's a new way of advocating atheism. Let's look at how these two contemporary atheists have employed this strategy.

RICHARD DAWKINS

Richard Dawkins is perhaps the world's best-known atheist at the moment. He is a British biologist and well-known spokesperson for atheism, and his preference for using this burden-of-proof strategy is clear. Atheists, he insists, have no obligation to bring reasons to support their position. Instead, it is up to those who believe God exists to present a convincing case for their position. The burden of proof lies squarely, and only, with theism. Dawkins goes so far as to call it a "favorite trick" of theists to call upon atheists to give reasons to believe there is no God. Interestingly, he concedes that such reasons are hard to come by but adds forcefully that to ask for such reasons for atheism is illegitimate since the burden of proof does not lie with atheism. In sum, atheists have no need to prove there is no God. It is the theist's job to prove there is one.[3]

DALE BEYERSTEIN'S SIMILAR ARGUMENT

Canadian philosopher Dale Beyerstein takes a similar approach in his own defense of atheism. In his view, atheism is the default viewpoint, pure and simple, which means atheists have no need to present arguments for their position. Their only job is to evaluate those presented by theists for God's existence and to explain why these arguments are not persuasive. In other words, the atheist is

3. Dawkins, *God Delusion*, 51–54.

on good grounds holding atheism even in the absence of any supporting reasons.[4]

WHY BURDEN OF PROOF MATTERS

Whatever we think of this new way of advocating atheism, we should not underestimate its power to change the entire discussion and to put atheism in a highly enviable position. Designating atheism as the default position dramatically reduces the atheist's job since no arguments are required. All atheists need to do is critique the arguments for theism and find them unconvincing. This is important because there are many ways of criticizing arguments for a viewpoint when those arguments are not being compared side-by-side with those for the opposing view. Poking holes in the arguments for any viewpoint is a fairly easy task for most of us and especially so for trained thinkers, far easier than evaluating arguments for different viewpoints to determine which are stronger.

For instance, a theistic argument may not attempt to prove God's existence with absolute certainty but simply to make a strong case for God. The atheist may claim this strategy, even if successful, leaves room for doubt. Or perhaps the arguments presented do not prove all the attributes the Judeo-Christian God is said to possess. Either way, so long as atheists are not convinced by the arguments they've heard for theism, they are justified in falling back to atheism even without providing arguments for it since it is regarded as the default position. Clearly, moving one's viewpoint into the default position gives it a significant leg up over any opposing position.

4. Beyerstein's position was articulated in a debate between himself and me held on the campus of Regent College, Vancouver, British Columbia, in January 1997.

HOW ATHEISM ATTAINED THIS ENVIABLE POSITION

Perhaps you're wondering how we got here. How did atheism attain this enviable position? Can atheists simply say it and make it so? Can you just name something and claim it? If not, what rationale do atheists offer for this game-changing claim that the burden of proof rests solely on theism?

Consider the reasons Zach, our philosophy of religion student, provides for this strategy when he is asked about it by his two colleagues, Emmanuel and Claire, as they meet at a local pub after class.

Claire. I need a drink!

Zach. Me too. My head always hurts after those philosophy lectures.

Claire. It's not the lecture I'm thinking about.

Zach. What then?

Claire. It's your idea that atheists have no need to support their view with reasons. Are you really sticking with that?

Zach. Of course!

Claire. So you get to sit here and do nothing to defend atheism, while Emmanuel does all the work defending theism?

Zach. Well I'm not sitting here doing nothing, but, yes.

Claire. As I said before, that's a nice convenient position you've worked out for yourself. I've got to hand it to you, but can you just say that and make it so?

Zach. It's not me who makes it true, and I don't care how convenient it is. As I said last time, it's the nature of atheism that makes it so.

Claire. And just how does it do that?

Zach. It's really not difficult. Let me show you just how simple it is. Have you heard of the tooth fairy?

Claire. Who hasn't?

Zach. Do you *believe* in the tooth fairy?

Emmanuel. Hey, why are we changing the subject?

Zach. Believe me, we're not. Well, Claire, do you?

Claire. (*Smirking.*) Well, there had to be someone putting the money under my pillow when I was a kid.

Zach. But do you believe in the tooth fairy now?

Claire. You sound like a real killjoy, but, no, I don't believe the tooth fairy exists. So what?

Zach. My point is, suppose you met someone who asked you to *give reasons* for your view that the tooth fairy does *not* exist. That is your position, after all. You are an a-toothfairyist.[5]

Claire. Is this what happens when a person reads too much philosophy?

Zach. Stick with me. If this person asked you to give reasons for your view that the tooth fairy does *not* exist, I'll bet you'd shake your head. You'd tell them the job of giving reasons belongs to the person who thinks the tooth fairy *does* exist, not to you. They're the one making the positive claim about the existence of something. Your claim is the negative one. It simply denies their claim."

Claire. (*Again smirking.*) Well, that relieves me of a serious responsibility since I am . . . what did you call me . . . an a-toothfairyist.

Zach. You can joke about it if you want but I'm just applying the same principle to the person who believes *God* does not exist. He's simply denying the theist's claim and, obviously, has no more duty to provide reasons for this position than the person who does not believe the tooth fairy exists. As I said, it's all pretty simple.

5. This term was used by Christopher Hitchens in his debate with William Lane Craig. His form of the word was "a-toothfairyism." See Biola University, "Does God Exist?," 1:06.

Zach is right about one thing. His line of reasoning is not difficult to grasp. It's the same one employed by my atheist counterpart in the debate mentioned earlier. It's also the one used by Dawkins, Beyerstein, and many others today as well. As my debate friend put it, we atheists are not the ones claiming something on the question of God's existence. We are simply denying the claim that God exists. There is nothing for us to prove.

To illustrate this approach he, along with Dawkins, Beyerstein, and many others, including Zach in the dialogue above, compare belief in God to belief in another group of characters whom we all agree are fictional: Mother Goose, Santa Claus, the tooth fairy, and even the celestial tea pot made famous by Bertrand Russell. In fact, the more one engages with atheists and their writings, the more one discovers how popular these fictional characters are.

Their reasoning is straightforward. Suppose you, like most of us, do *not* believe in the actual existence of the tooth fairy, Santa Claus, or Mother Goose. Are you thereby *obligated* to produce arguments or proofs for your position that these characters do *not* exist? Of course not, you will be told. Such a demand would be entirely unreasonable and should be met with a headshake. That obligation belongs to anyone who claims these characters *do* exist. And, says the atheist, the same principle applies to the person who does not believe God exists.[6] What can be said about this way of looking at things? It's the question we turn to now.

6. Dawkins, *God Delusion*, 51–54.

Chapter 5

Is There a Default Position?

As you can imagine, not all theists have been content to stand by and accept atheism as the default position, or theism as the view which bears the full burden of proof. In fact, as shocking as it may be to some atheists, plenty of theists contend that if there is a default view on the question of God's existence, it is theism, not atheism. In my own lectures and interactions with both groups, I have discovered repeatedly that many people in both groups take it for granted that their stance should be the default one. If you happen to be an atheist reading these pages, chances are you're wondering how anyone could, with a straight face, think theism is the default position. After all, doesn't theism put forward the truth claim on this question? Isn't it the one with something to prove?

Notice the reason Emmanuel provides for thinking that maybe theism should be the default position as he presents it to a shocked Zach in their next meeting at the university pub:

Zach. You called this meeting right, Emmanuel?

Emmanuel. I wouldn't be so formal about it, but, yes, I thought of a few things since our last conversation and wanted to get your take on them.

Zach. I have to admit, you seemed a little unsettled when we left last time.

Emmanuel. Well, I have to admit I'm not so sure about your idea that atheism is the default position, the one you can fall back to even if you haven't proved it.

Zach. First, it's not just my idea. Have you forgotten about the tooth fairy? It's obvious that atheism is the default position since it is not the view making the claim here. Atheism is simply the denial of your claim.

Emmanuel. Obvious to some people, maybe.

Zach. What are you getting at here, Emmanuel?

Emmanuel. I actually think it could be the other way round.

Zach. What could be the other way around?

Emmanuel. Theism just might be the default position, not atheism.

Zach. (*Slowly lowering his drink.*) That's unbelievable!

Emmanuel. Maybe not. Think of it this way. When any of us sees an object, say a picture on the wall or a screwdriver or machine, we never assume the item popped into existence uncaused, out of nothing. We always assume that some person or something made it. Am I correct?

Zach. Okay, and what is that supposed to show?

Emmanuel. It shows how deeply we all believe a very well-known principle.

Zach. Which is?

Emmanuel. *Ex nihilo, nihil fit.*

Zach. Yes, out of nothing, nothing comes.

Emmanuel. That's right. Even if people have not heard the phrase in Latin, as you have, they still follow it in the rest of their lives. It's a foundational principle in all of science, philosophy, politics, and just about everywhere else. It's nothing more than a recognition that things do not pop into existence uncaused, out of nothing. If something came into being, it had a cause. We almost never feel the need to explain or defend this principle. Rather, we reason *from* it to many other ideas.

ZACH. (*Shaking his head.*) I see where you're going here but why don't you spell it out.

EMMANUEL. (*Chuckling.*) It's simple really, to quote a friend of mine. If things don't pop into existence out of nothing, then universes don't come out of nothing either. They, too, must be caused by something powerful enough to do the job. That's what theists claim.

ZACH. I saw that coming.

EMMANUEL. I'm sure you did, but let's not miss the best part. This is why some of us think the burden of proof is on people who think the universe had *no* cause, just as it would be on someone who thought a screwdriver or computer popped into existence uncaused.

ZACH. So you are actually implying that theism should be the default position?

EMMANUEL. Well, it does fit with the well-known maxim we just mentioned: "Out of nothing, nothing comes."

As surprising as this sounds to some atheists, like Zach in the dialogue, one does not need to be a Christian, or even a theist, to see why some people think theism should be the default position, the one to fall back into in the absence of decisive arguments for the opposing view. In fact, even Kai Nielsen, a prolific and well-respected atheist philosopher, in a discussion about God's existence, once asked an audience to consider how they would respond to someone telling them a loud bang they heard outside the room was not caused by anything at all but just happened. He then stated the obvious, that none of them would accept such an explanation. They would consider that response to be "quite unintelligible," he said.[1]

1. This illustration was used in a public debate between atheist philosopher Kai Nielsen and Christian philosopher William Lane Craig on the topic of "God, Morality, and Evil" at the University of Western Ontario, February 1991.

Theism simply claims that Nielsen's answer applies not only to little bangs but to big ones too. It would be no more intelligible to believe the entire universe came into existence from nothing than to believe a small bang outside the lecture theatre did. Theism asserts that someone brought the universe into existence; it did not just happen, and it's not difficult to see why more than a few people regard it as the default position.

IS THE BURDEN OF PROOF ALWAYS ON THE POSITIVE CLAIM?

What about the widely held assumption, however, that the burden of proof is always on the positive? According to it, people making *positive* claims (including theists) need to support and defend their claims but those making *negative* ones do not. If true, it elevates atheism to the default position regardless of the comments above by Kai Nielsen. It is an assumption I've encountered often in my own conversations on this issue. It is taken to be as obvious as the claim that 2 + 2 = 4, and any questioning of it is met with a blank look.

What is behind this assumption? Is it really so obvious? Notice how the discussion goes when Emmanuel and Zach press deeper into this question.

Emmanuel. If I may say so, Zach, you were the one who seemed a little agitated at the end of our last conversation.

Zach. Well, when you drop a bombshell like that, what do you expect? Whoever heard of the idea that the burden of proof might actually be on atheism?

Emmanuel. Obviously not you, but I know a lot of people who have.

Zach. All your religious friends, I suppose?

Emmanuel. And a few others too.

Zach. As far as I'm concerned, it's still a huge stretch to think of theism as the default position. I mean, really!?

EMMANUEL. Then you may be interested in another option, one we haven't mentioned yet.

ZACH. How can there be a third option? There are only two views here. Doesn't one of them have to be the default position?

EMMANUEL. I'm not sure about you but the more we talk about it, the more I wonder how either of these views could be the default position. How does either get to claim this status? Both are making important claims about the universe so shouldn't both support their claims?

ZACH. But atheism is making a negative claim and theism, a positive one.

EMMANUEL. Sure but a negative assertion is still an assertion, is it not? Holocaust deniers are asserting the Holocaust never happened. Anti-vaxxers are asserting COVID-19 vaccines were unhelpful at best. Atheists are asserting there is no God. Both theism and atheism are making big truth claims, which means we have an even playing field here.

ZACH. Are you saying it makes no difference whether claims are positive or negative?

EMMANUEL. Oh, it makes a big difference in what they are asserting, but it doesn't change the fact that they're both still claims. And the negative claim you're making is a rather big one, don't you think? You're asserting there is no God anywhere in or out of the universe. Do you know how much knowledge it would require for someone to know that back behind the things science observes, there is no supernatural divine being? You'd need way more knowledge than humans have. What's more, as we said earlier, there is a universe sitting here. Atheism seems to violate the principle, out of nothing, nothing comes.

ZACH. My claim is no bigger than the one you're making.

EMMANUEL. Agreed. We're both making big claims. It's an even playing field.

Emmanuel's contention in this dialogue is that a negative truth claim is still a truth claim. It is not accurate to say atheism makes no truth claim. Both theism and atheism make important truth claims. Interestingly, this is not something recognized only by Christians or theists. The well respected atheist Bertrand Russell clearly acknowledged that atheism's claim, while negative, is a genuine claim to know something. Recall his definition earlier in which he said the Christian holds that we can know there is a God, while the atheist holds we can know there is not. Both are claims to know something important.

This is why Kai Nielsen, the atheist philosopher mentioned earlier, has also argued that atheists need to provide reasons for their position just as theists do for theirs. His further explanation of this requirement is as clear as it is candid:

> If the arguments for the existence of God are shown to be unsound, it does not *follow* that God does not exist. . . . To show that an argument is invalid or unsound is not to show that the *conclusion of the argument is false*, . . . only . . . that the argument does not warrant our asserting the conclusion to be true. All the proofs of God's existence may fail, but it still may be the case that God exists. . . . In short, to show that the proofs do not work is not enough, by itself. . . . It still may be the case that there is a God.[2]

Nielsen's point is that atheism, like theism, cannot be defended by simply rebutting arguments for the opposing position. It requires its own separate arguments. Atheism, he says, is in the same epistemic boat as theism. If the atheist were able to show that every argument for theism was unsound, he would still only have shown that the arguments in support of theism fail. He would not have shown atheism to be true. Without separate arguments for atheism, he writes, for all he knows there could still be a God. It is careful thinking coming from a thoughtful atheist philosopher.

We could add that it is no defense of atheism to merely announce that one is not personally convinced by the arguments one has heard for theism, or any other viewpoint for that matter. That

2. Nielsen, *Reason and Practice*, 143–44.

statement is nothing more than a comment about one's own state of mind and says little about the strength or weakness of the arguments presented. It's a comment about the person making it, not really about the arguments.

BUT WHAT ABOUT THOSE FICTIONAL CHARACTERS?

If we are correct that neither theism nor atheism is the default position, it still leaves an intriguing question. What about those fictional characters we talked about earlier: Santa Claus, the tooth fairy, Mother Goose, the flying teapot, and the others? Recall that many atheists point to these characters and argue that just as people who do *not* believe they exist have no obligation to prove their nonexistence, neither do atheists have a duty to support their view that God does not exist. That job would belong to someone who claimed they *did* exist.

What are we to make of this reasoning? Do atheists have a point here? Notice what happens when Zach and Emmanuel explore this question.

Zach. (*Spotting Emmanuel hurrying across campus.*) Hey, Emmanuel, got a minute?

Emmanuel. (*Turning quickly and stopping.*) I'm just heading to the library for some last-minute review before my next class. This professor likes pop quizzes on his assigned readings.

Zach. Did you get my text?

Emmanuel. (*Quickly checking his phone.*) I see it here now. So you have a question you wanted to talk about?

Zach. Yes, if you have a minute.

Emmanuel. (*Motioning Zach to sit with him in a group of library chairs.*) Is it something I said . . . or did?

Zach. Actually, it's something you left out.

Emmanuel. Hmm. What was that?

Zach. Last time we talked, you suggested that maybe neither atheism nor theism is the default position.

Emmanuel. You're right, I did.

Zach. But didn't you forget the tooth fairy?

Emmanuel. How could I forget the tooth fairy when you keep mentioning her. You seem to have taken quite an interest in her recently.

Zach. Well it does seem like you ignored the point I made about her. You said atheism is not the default position because atheists are making a truth claim, just like theists.

Emmanuel. Yes, atheists claim that God does not exist.

Zach. But are you really telling me that someone who believes there is no tooth fairy has to prove that? Surely you can't be saying that.

Emmanuel. Here is exactly what I'm saying. Negative claims are still claims. We already talked about that. And because they're claims, they need to be proven or supported. So now the only question is *why* we don't ask tooth fairy deniers to prove their view.

Zach. That's easy. Because their view is a negative claim.

Emmanuel. I don't think so. Negative claims are still claims, and claims need to be supported. People who deny the Holocaust ever occurred, or that vaccines are effective, still need to support those claims. Let me suggest a different reason.

Zach. Which is . . . ?

Emmanuel. Before I say it, have you ever noticed that you, and other atheists, always use fictional fun characters like the tooth fairy or Mother Goose as their examples when they argue that the burden of proof is on theism? Atheists never use real life figures or events.

Zach. Now that you mention it, I suppose I have.

EMMANUEL. I doubt that's a coincidence. Let me suggest that atheists are sticking with these fictional characters because their reasoning only works with them. And the reason it works is simply because no one ever believed these characters existed in the first place, except children whose parents are putting money under the pillow. But as soon as they grow older, they figure it out and join in the fun too. The point is that since everyone already knows they are fun and fictional, no one is asking anyone to prove they don't exist.

ZACH. Are you sure about this?

EMMANUEL. Well, watch what happens to this reasoning by atheists if we replace these fictional characters with normal objects, the kind we all experience day-to-day, and try out the same argument. Imagine instead of telling us you do not believe in tooth fairies or Santa Claus, you told us you did not believe in bacteria or that astronauts had ever landed on the moon. Or for something more important, suppose you told us you didn't believe the Holocaust happened or the COVID-19 virus were real, that they were both hoaxes foisted upon the world.

ZACH. Like my neighbor. He denies the COVID-19 virus was real, but I've never been convinced by his arguments.

EMMANUEL. Well, suppose your neighbor went further and argued that since his claim about the virus is a negative one, it is not his job to give any arguments for it. That job belongs to you since you think the virus *is* real? Here's the question: Does the fact that a person's belief about a normal object or event like this is negative eliminate the need for them to give reasons for them?

ZACH. I think we all know your answer.

EMMANUEL. It's not just my answer. It does not, and I think we realize it. If you deny the existence of normal everyday objects or events, you need to give reasons for thinking they don't exist. And this shows that the burden of proof is not eliminated because a claim is negative, but only when the claim is about something fictitious and fun, when everyone already knows it does not exist.

Zach. (*Checking his watch.*) Hey, we've got to get to class. So much for your prep for that pop quiz.

This dialogue is drawing attention to the real reason we do not ask people to prove the tooth fairy does not exist. It is not because their claim about tooth fairies is negative but rather because no one ever thought tooth fairies did exist, so of course, we're not asking anyone to prove they do not.

In case one doubts this, notice two things. First, note that the examples atheists use in arguing this way are always characters which everyone knows are fictional pretend ones, like the tooth fairy, Santa, Mother Goose, the spaghetti monster, or Bertrand Russell's flying teapot. As Emmanuel noted in the dialogue, this is not a coincidence. It is because the reasoning only works with such fictional figures. And it works simply because no one thought they existed in the first place, not because their claim is negative.[3]

Second, we should notice what happens to this reasoning if we replace these fictional characters with common nonfictional ones as Emmanuel did. It collapses immediately. Imagine someone informing you that they do not believe the African country of Burkina Faso exists (it is a clever hoax by the media), or the COVID-19 virus was real, or that Mussolini was a real person. If they then argued that since these claims are all negative ones, they have no duty to give reasons for them, they would not get far. We recognize that negative claims about real-life matters are still claims which need to be supported, in some cases more so than their positive counterpart claims. It is fair for others to ask why they believe their assertions, and if they want to be taken seriously, they will come prepared with a few reasons.

This still leaves an important question, namely, whether God is like the tooth fairy. If you have engaged with atheists, you will

3. See Chamberlain, *Why People Don't Believe*, 82–83, for a fuller explanation of the distinction between negativity and triviality and the impact of both on the question of burden of proof.

know that in the view of many, God has precisely the status of a fictional character and should be taken no more seriously than the tooth fairy or Santa.[4] So, of course, it follows that the atheist has no more burden of proof than someone who denies the existence of these fictional characters. Again, do people who reason this way have a point?

IS GOD LIKE THE TOOTH FAIRY?

What kind of character is God? Many atheists refer to God as just one more fictional character which should be taken no more seriously than the tooth fairy or Santa. So, of course, in their minds, the atheist would have no more duty to prove God's nonexistence than someone who denies the existence of these fictional characters. The key question then is this: Is the concept of God a trivial or inconsequential one like the tooth fairy or Santa, or is it a serious normal concept on a par with other normal ideas like the existence of Mussolini or the Holocaust or even everyday objects like trees, buildings, or baseball bats?

Perhaps this seems like a difficult or debatable question, one which we all must settle by thinking about how we feel about the concept of God. But is this question really that open or difficult? Is belief in God really like belief in the tooth fairy? Hardly? All one need do is consider the astonishing effects the belief in God, and also the rejection of this belief, have led to in our world throughout history.

People's views about God have driven them to change their live's directions, to write books and articles arguing their case, to travel around the world to attend conferences, to die, and even to kill. Ironically, new atheists are perhaps in the weakest position to argue belief in God is trivial and should be compared to belief in the tooth fairy since, in their view, this belief leads to violence, intolerance, and an assortment of other evils. Of course, plenty of others disagree and are convinced that belief in God leads to

4. Richard Dawkins articulates this viewpoint in an interview which can be viewed in Theworldvideos1, "Richard Dawkins."

peace, forgiveness, harmony, and hope. Either way, it is hard to imagine a more consequential belief. The point is that the question of God's existence has been anything but a trifling or trivial matter throughout history, and any comparison of it to Mother Goose or the tooth fairy is an extreme stretch.

The advice from Kai Nielsen, stated above, should not be forgotten. Both theism and atheism declare something significant about our world and universe, hence neither should be considered the default view. It is hard to avoid his conclusion that proponents of both views need to bring forward supporting reasons for their viewpoints.

Does this settle the matter then? It might seem so, but one further strategy for placing the burden of proof solely on theism needs to be unpacked. It involves intricate distinctions which can be difficult to detect and follow. It even involves a change in the way atheism itself is defined. We are now in a position to look into this strategy.

Chapter 6

Strategy #2: Redefining Atheism

EARLIER WE NOTED BERTRAND Russell's standard traditional definition of atheism. The atheist, he said, claims to know God does not exist. It's a clear and simple definition. In recent times, however, this clear definition of atheism has grown fuzzy as a number of atheists have begun to speak of it in different ways. The new language is subtle and sometimes hard to detect, but the consequences for how the discussion goes from there are far-reaching. Notice Zach's conversation-stopping way of defining atheism when pressed by Claire for a clear definition in their next rendezvous.

CLAIRE. So, can we finally agree that negative claims, including atheism's assertion that God does not exist, are still claims that need to be supported?

ZACH. Actually, that depends.

CLAIRE. On . . . ?

ZACH. It depends on what the person means when making a negative claim.

CLAIRE. (*Shaking her head ever so slightly.*) I guess it's too much to hope for a straight answer. You've got to love philosophy.

ZACH. Well, people could mean more than one thing when they say they don't believe there is a God.

CLAIRE. Like what?

ZACH. One person might be saying he believes there is no God, but someone else might just be saying he does not believe there is a God.

CLAIRE. Hey, didn't you just say the same thing there twice?

ZACH. No. One person believes God does not exist. The other person simply does not believe God does exist.

CLAIRE. (*Throws up her hands.*) And you're saying there's a difference between those two?

ZACH. Yes, an important one. The first person is telling us something he believes. He believes God does not exist. The second person is not stating a belief or claim at all. He is telling us something he does *not* believe. He does *not* believe God does exist. Period. End of story. The first person was stating a belief, the second person was not.

EMMANUEL. You've got to be kidding me!

CLAIRE. I don't think he is kidding, Emmanuel.

ZACH. You're right, I'm not. I'm clarifying my position. As an atheist, I simply don't believe God exists. I'm telling you something I don't believe and, as such, am not making a claim at all.

EMMANUEL. (*Mutters under his breath and turns away.*)

Perhaps you find this to be a case of meaningless philosophical hairsplitting. For atheists who make this distinction, however, it is of utmost importance and a matter of serious discussion in the literature. Recall the earlier statement by new atheist Christopher Hitchens in which he made clear that he had no intention of bringing reasons to show that God did not exist. His basis for his atheism consisted entirely in his claim that there were no convincing reasons to believe God does exist. What we may miss is that embedded in this way of defending atheism is a particular definition of atheism, one which is very different from the one given by Bertrand Russell. Atheism, by definition, is a position which does not require supporting arguments. How can this be?

In the debate in which I participated, mentioned earlier, one of the atheist debaters had asserted forcefully that the burden of proof was always on the person making the positive claim, and therefore, they, the atheist debaters, had no need to bring supporting reasons for their position.

As the debate went on, I decided to ask whether he was willing to stand by this claim. His response could not have been clearer. He reemphasized his belief that people who make positive claims are *always* the ones required to prove their claims, while those who make negative ones have no need to do so.

No one in that room doubted where my atheist friend stood on the matter . . . except me. I still wondered if he was really prepared to be consistent with this principle all the way through. To find out, I presented him with a specific negative assertion—"The Holocaust never happened"—and asked whether he thought someone who made this negative assertion really had no need to bring supporting reasons for it. Here is when the new way of portraying atheism began to appear. After thinking for a couple of seconds, he carefully distinguished between the two assertions mentioned in the dialogue above. The assertions were these:

First assertion: I believe the Holocaust did not occur.

Second assertion: I do not believe the Holocaust occurred.

You may want to read them again to spot the difference between them. My atheist friend agreed that a person making the first assertion would need to bring supporting reasons for it because he was stating something he believed to be true, namely, that the Holocaust did not happen. This was something of a backtrack since he was now admitting that for some negative claims (like the first one above), there *is* a burden of proof required after all, namely, claims in which a person asserts something they believe to be true. I understood it to be a clarification of his position.

It was his understanding of the second assertion, however, that really caught my attention. A person making it, he said, would have no need to support it since it was not a statement of belief.

That person was merely declaring their *lack of belief* that the Holocaust happened.

Of course, the Holocaust was not our main concern that evening, and my friend then applied the same distinction to the issue at hand—the existence of God. On this issue, he made the same distinction between these two statements:

First statement: I believe God does not exist.

Second statement: I do not believe God exists.

Here again, you may need to read these statements over a couple of times to see the difference, and even then, you may regard them as simply two ways of saying the same thing. Most of us would use them interchangeably and mean the same thing by them, but they were not the same at all according to our atheist friends that evening.

At this point the new portrayal of atheism was on full display and was captured in the second statement above. Atheism was being defined as nothing more than a lack of belief in God's existence. It involved no truth claim and therefore no need to support one. That was purely the theist's job.

As noted earlier, the definition of atheism has become an area of focus and discussion. It is of great importance for plenty of atheists and a matter under discussion in the literature. Stephen Bullivant, coauthor of *The Oxford Handbook of Atheism*, states that the task of finding "the precise definition of 'atheism' is both a vexed and vexatious issue."[1]

Furthermore, even a quick purview of the literature makes clear that our atheist friends in the debate, are not alone in defining atheism as a lack of belief in the existence of God. In the opening chapter of *The Oxford Handbook of Atheism*, Bullivant surveys a number of definitions and understandings of atheism while explaining and justifying *The Handbook's* own definition as "the absence of belief in the existence of a God or gods."[2]

1. Bullivant, "Defining Atheism," 11.
2. Bullivant, "Defining Atheism," 16, 20.

In advocating this definition, Bullivant is joined by many others including New Zealand's well-known journalist and lecturer Brian Edwards, who argues against any meaningful distinction between atheism and agnosticism and defines an atheist simply as someone who does not believe in the existence of God.[3] In other words, an atheist need not deny the existence of God. All that is required is to lack belief in God.

The popular television personality and magician Penn Jillette defines his own atheism similarly in the following words: "If I don't know, I don't believe. . . . I'm not going to use faith to fill in the gaps."[4] In a conversation with a group of Christian pastors, he once spoke positively of his own experience of attending a church which had a smart and wonderful pastor but claimed that he, Jillette, lacked the knowledge necessary to know there is a God. He simply did not know and therefore self-identified as an atheist.[5]

Bullivant's justification for this definition centers on the parallel between the Greek negating prefix *a* and the English prefix "un." He argues that just as the English prefix "un" negates words like "necessary," "tie," "belief," and many others, the Greek prefix *a* signifies a simple absence or lack or "state of being without."[6] Atheism, he says, "thus becomes an absence of something called 'theism.'"[7] Most importantly, he adds, "It does not require a specific denial or rejection of, nor any animus against, this 'theism'—although, also importantly, it does not rule it out."[8]

Even Bullivant, however, concedes that this is not a strong reason for choosing this definition. Greek usage, he notes, was "variable." He illustrates this variation by citing the Greek word *atheos* which, he notes, could "connote 'one who denies or dishonours

3. Brian Edwards stated this definition and understanding of atheism in a live radio debate with William Lane Craig on April 16, 2011. See Drcraigvideos, "Great Easter Debate," 2:23.

4. Kain, "Penn Jillette on Atheism."

5. The Preachers, "Penn Jillette Explains."

6. Bullivant, "Defining Atheism," 13.

7. Bullivant, "Defining Atheism," 14.

8. Bullivant, "Defining Atheism," 14.

the God' (as used of Socrates in Plato's Apology), a sense that goes beyond a simple, privative absence of belief."[9]

In any case, says Bullivant, we can only draw so much from the meaning of this Greek prefix or even the Greek meaning of atheism. It has been an English word for over four and a half centuries and has its own extended tradition of understanding, which has quite consistently demanded, "not merely an absence of theism, but instead a definite rejection of it." As an example of a definition in keeping with this tradition, he cites McGrath's definition which is "a principled and informed decision to reject belief in God."[10]

The upshot of it all is that if atheism is defined as simply the lack of belief in God, atheists are in the enviable position of simply having to show up and point out reasons why they are not convinced by the arguments for theism. As noted earlier, there are many ways of finding the arguments for a viewpoint to be weak or inconclusive or not as strong as we would like them to be when they are not being compared with the arguments for an opposing position. What are we to make of this definition of atheism?

9. Bullivant, "Defining Atheism," 14.

10. McGrath's definition is cited and analyzed in Bullivant, "Defining Atheism," 14.

Chapter 7

The Changing Definition of Atheism: A Response

Is IT REALLY THAT easy to change the definition of a view as old and established as atheism such that it is now the mere absence of belief?

TRIVIALIZING ATHEISM

William Lane Craig has argued that this definition actually trivializes atheism. It undermines it as a genuine viewpoint or position at all. To say atheism is only the absence of belief, says Craig, turns it into nothing more than a psychological state of an individual person. As such, it can be neither true nor false in the way that theism or atheism defined as the denial of God's existence can.

If atheism is nothing more than the absence of belief in God, Craig continues, it means that anyone who has not thought the matter through and come to the intentional belief in God, including babies and young children, are now atheists.[1]

This should give us pause when considering turning from the long-standing traditional definition of atheism stated by Bertrand Russell, Kai Nielsen, and found in a host of encyclopedias and dictionaries of philosophy including the *Encyclopedia of Philosophy*,

1. See comments by Craig in Reasonable Faith, "Atheism Shmatheism."

Academic American Encyclopedia, Oxford Companion to Philosophy, and others.[2]

CLARIFYING ATHEISM'S NEW DEFINITION

A further question should be raised about this definition of atheism and the reasoning behind it. What, exactly, does it mean? Is the statement "I do not believe there is a God" really only a statement of nonbelief, or is someone who makes it expressing a point of view just as with the first statement? If so, what exactly is that view?

How does one wade into a conversation with an atheist who makes this distinction? Note how Claire decides to press Zach on this question

Claire. Well, Zach, you're inventive, I'll give you that.

Zach. Thanks, but what did I invent?

Claire. Your distinction between believing there is no God and not believing there is one.

Zach. First of all, I didn't invent the distinction, and secondly, it's real. Those statements are different. Importantly different.

Claire. Well, I have to admit you had me stumped . . . at first that is, but then I wondered, couldn't Emmanuel play the same game?

Zach. What game?

Claire. Couldn't he just define theism as a lack of belief too?

Zach. How could he? Theism is the belief that God exists. That's a positive claim, end of story.

2. See the following YouTube video where William Lane Craig lists a large number of encyclopedias and dictionaries of philosophy, religion, etc., including the *Academic American Encyclopedia, Random House Encyclopedia, Oxford Companion to Philosophy, Dictionary of Philosophy, World Book Encyclopedia, Encyclopedia of Philosophy*, and *Encyclopedia of Religion* to demonstrate the wide consistency in the definition of atheism as the intentional denial of God's existence. Drcraigvideos, "Atheism Redefined."

Claire. Actually, it would be pretty easy if he just followed your definition but flipped it. Instead of saying he believes God exists, Emmanuel could just say to you, "You say God doesn't exist, but I don't believe that." He would just be telling you something he does not believe. He could even go further and tell you that he could never accept your claim that God does not exist because, as he likes to say, how could anyone know that back behind the things science observes, there is no supernatural being.

Emmanuel. Yes, bring it.

Claire. My point is that, if he said that, isn't he the one who now lacks belief? He just doesn't believe God does not exist. Wouldn't that mean he now has no need to bring arguments for his view?

Emmanuel. That's ingenious, Claire. Why didn't I think of that?

Zach. You may think it's alright, Emmanuel, but I wouldn't accept that for a minute. No atheist would.

Claire. That's very interesting. I was just about to say that. No atheist would accept it. In fact, I'm sure they would be asking theists to quit playing games with double negatives and to come right out and say what they *do* believe, not what they don't. Am I right?

Zach. That and a few other things.

Claire. And it would be a fair comment. My only question is why the same comment shouldn't be made to any atheist who has portrayed atheism as a purely negative view. We all know atheism's claim is negative but it's still a claim, and we're more interested in what atheists *do* believe than what they don't.

Emmanuel. I think she has a point, Zach.

Zach. Of course you do.

The preceding dialogue highlights the critical feature of recent strategies for advancing atheism, i.e., the distinction between the following two statements, along with the insistence that atheism involves the second, not the first:

1. I believe there is no God.
2. I do not believe there is a God.

This, allegedly, frees an atheist from any burden of proof since atheism is now strictly a statement of nonbelief in the existence of God. The burden of proof rests entirely with theists who believe there is a God. The question is whether this is a successful strategy.

To evaluate it, let's ask the question mentioned in the preceding dialogue.

CAN TWO PLAY THIS GAME?

This question was raised to me by a group of my graduate students when I put this new way of defining atheism to them. It was a question I had not thought of. Couldn't theists play the same game as atheists, they asked. When I pressed them for an explanation, one replied that atheists are not the only ones who could define their position negatively. Why couldn't theists do that too? Instead of declaring that God exists, he asked, why couldn't theists define their position this way: "We theists do not believe God does *not* exist. Our claim is strictly negative. We're no longer claiming to believe something; theism is now simply a lack of belief. It's a denial of atheism which claims that God does not exist so, of course, we are not the ones who need to bring any arguments for our view. That's the atheist's job since they are the ones claiming to believe something, namely, that God does not exist."

This elicited a few chuckles among the other students, and it was obvious the student had said it tongue in cheek. At the same time, the student was trying to make a point. The atheist strategy could be played both ways. Even though theism's claim is positive and atheism's negative, both views make important truth claims. Each position, then, could define itself as simply the denial of the other's claim. Furthermore, in the view of these students at least, this strategy was no more unreasonable one way than the other.

After further discussion, my students agreed that no atheist they had ever spoken with would accept this negative definition of theism, nor should they. That, however, was part of the point they were making. The atheist would probably reply, "You're only telling us what you do *not* believe. We're more interested in what you *do*." It would be a fair point, but it raises the question why the same comment should not be made to an atheist. "Atheism is making an important claim, too, so why not tell us what you do believe?" It would be a call to atheists to stick with the plain definition of atheism given by Bertrand Russell which, as we have seen, acknowledges that atheism claims to know something important about the universe.

REMOVING THE AMBIGUITY: WHAT THIS DEFINITION REALLY MEANS

A more important question needs to be asked about this way of defining atheism, namely, what it actually amounts to when we take a close look. What does it really mean to say one does not believe God exists versus saying one does believe God does not exist? Is it as clear as its proponents seem to think? Notice Zach's responses when Claire explores this question with him.

Claire. I think there's a far more important question you need to answer, Zach.

Zach. And I'm sure I'm about to hear it too.

Claire. I'm wondering what exactly you mean when you insist you do not believe there is a God.

Zach. Isn't it obvious?

Claire. Actually, I think the statement "I do not believe there is a God" is ambiguous. It needs to be clarified.

Zach. Clarified? How?

Claire. Well, when you say you do not believe there is a God, do you also not believe there is *no* God? Do you just not believe either way?

Zach. (*Frowning slightly.*) That sounds like a trick question to me.

Claire. Not at all. You've been telling us your definition of atheism is not a statement of what you do believe, but only of what you don't. It's a statement of nonbelief.

Zach. Yes!

Claire. You make no truth claim.

Zach. Correct.

Claire. You simply lack belief on the issue of God's existence.

Zach. Precisely!

Claire. Well, what I'm asking is, are you really lacking belief on the issue all the way around? Are you saying you do not believe there is a God and also saying you do not believe there is *no* God? You simply do not believe either way?

Zach. Well, if you want an answer, it is yes. As I've been saying from the beginning, my position involves no statement of belief.

Claire. So let me get this straight. You don't believe there *is a God*, and you also don't believe there is *not a God*. You're withholding belief on the question of God's existence.

Zach. Correct.

Claire. Well, that certainly clarifies your position, but shouldn't I be welcoming you to my side, the agnostic camp? You're now espousing agnosticism, not atheism anymore. In fact, it would be hard to state my view more clearly than you have just done. You don't believe either that there is or is not a God. So welcome!

Zach. (*Pausing momentarily.*) I'd like to change my answer.

Claire. Hmm. Changing answers midstream?

EMMANUEL. We may all need that freedom once in a while.

CLAIRE. Well, then, back to my question, Zach. When you say you do not believe there is a God, do you also not believe there is *no* God? You simply do not believe either way?

ZACH. After thinking about this, my new answer is no, that is not my position. When I say I don't believe God exists, I am not saying I also don't believe God does *not* exist. In fact, that is precisely what I do believe, namely, that God does not exist. I'm an atheist.

CLAIRE. (*Pauses.*) Wow! Did you just say what I think you said?

ZACH. That depends on what you think I said.

CLAIRE. This is quite a moment, Zach, because, unless I'm mistaken, you've just turned your back on everything you've been saying about your position.

ZACH. How have I done that?

CLAIRE. You've been telling us from the beginning that your position involves no statement of belief. You simply do not believe God exists. But now you just finished saying that you do believe God does not exist after all. That's your position. Which means you're back to defining atheism the old-fashioned way. It's the belief that God does not exist. I agree, but you know what that means, don't you?

ZACH. I can hear it coming.

CLAIRE. It means your position involves a claim, namely that God does not exist, and it needs to be supported just like any other truth claim would. You and Emmanuel are in the same boat. You are both making truth claims, and big ones too. He believes God exists. You believe God does not exist.

As the preceding discussion makes clear, the statement "I do not believe there is a God" is not as clear as it may look. In fact, it contains a deep ambiguity which needs clarification. A person who makes this statement is technically withholding belief on the issue. He simply does not believe there is a God. But a clarifying question should be put to a person who says this: When you say you do not believe there is a God, do you also not believe there is no God? Do you simply not believe either way? In other words, are you truly withholding belief on the issue?

As the preceding dialogue showed, there are two possible replies someone can give. First, one could reply by saying, "Yes, that is my view. I do not believe there is a God, and I also do not believe there is not one. I don't believe either way. My position involves no truth claim."

This response would certainly clear up the matter but notice it also means this person has abandoned atheism altogether and is now embracing agnosticism. This is a highly significant result. In fact, as Claire pointed out in the dialogue above, it would be hard to find a clearer statement of agnosticism than this. It's why Claire welcomed Zach into her camp when he at first took this approach.

Suppose, however, the atheist, not wanting to espouse agnosticism, goes the other way and says, "I do not believe God does exist, and I do believe he does not."

Notice what has happened with this answer. In taking this approach, the atheist has now reverted back to the traditional definition of atheism, the one put forward by Bertrand Russell and many others. He is now advocating the first of the two statements set out above, i.e., I believe God does not exist.

When Zach switched his position in the preceding dialogue and took this approach, it was a "Wow!" moment for Claire. And there is a bill to pay for it too. This traditional definition of atheism—"I believe God does not exist"—involves a truth claim and thus needs to be supported like any other truth claim.

WHERE HAVE WE COME?

The recent atheist strategy we have been examining has been to shift the burden of proof entirely to theism. It has revolved around a definition of atheism as *not believing God exists.* As we have seen, however, once we clarify the meaning and implications of this new definition, it leads to two possible options, both of which are problematic. One leads to the abandonment of atheism and the embrace of agnosticism instead. The other leads back to the traditional definition of atheism, namely the claim to believe there is no God, one which needs to be supported like any other truth claim.

Perhaps you're wondering if this all sounds like needless hairsplitting over terminology or of distinctions without much of a difference. In actuality, pursuing these careful definitions and distinctions involves doing nothing more than pressing our atheist friends to state their view—atheism—as clearly and transparently as atheists have done throughout history and to recognize the need to bring supporting reasons for it, just as theists do.

In the current climate, it has become necessary to ask atheists if they still agree with atheism's historic claim that God does not exist. If they hesitate in answering this question, then we need to find out whether their position is really atheism at all. If someone claims to believe there is no God, then he is indeed asserting the traditional atheism and needs to bring forward reasons to believe it. If, on the other hand, someone merely claims not to believe either that there is or is not a God, then he is withholding belief on the question and, as such, is now endorsing agnosticism. Atheism has been abandoned.

Chapter 8

What Does This Mean for My Conversations?

In the previous chapter, we saw that when atheism is defined simply as not believing there is a God, it is ambiguous and needs to be clarified. Once that is done, an important question arises: Why does this matter? Simply put, it does because the difference between atheism and agnosticism matters. As we noted earlier in this book, conversations with atheists can be very different from those with agnostics because this difference in viewpoint can affect the interest or openness people have in searching for God. If you truly believe something does not exist, you will not spend much time looking for it. Why look for something you know is not there? If, however, you are not sure, you just might.

We may inform our atheist friends as passionately as we want about the severe implications of ignoring God if there is one, but if they are convinced God isn't there, they will have no concern. It's all a fairy tale. Agnostics, on the other hand, just might search for God because, for all they know, one might exist. The implications of ignoring God may not be so quickly set aside by them. These differences matter for our conversations.

The upshot of this is that we all, theists and atheists alike, would be unwise to set aside atheist philosopher Kai Nielsen's earlier instruction. Atheism, he reminded us, just like theism, involves an actual belief, namely, that there is no God. As such, it requires its own evidence or argument in support just as theism does. It is not sufficient for an atheist to simply fall back to atheism as the default position and claim that his only job is to evaluate theistic arguments to see if they are convincing.

We should press all parties in the discussion over God's existence to bring forward supporting reasons for their claims. Atheists assert that beyond this universe, beyond the things science observes, there is no divine supernatural being. Theists claim such a divine being does exist. Few claims have wider implications for our lives and other important views, as a perusal of most introductory philosophy textbooks will show.

Where have we come so far? We have been examining creative strategies by which atheism is elevated to the enviable position of the default view, thus making the job of defending it far simpler. These have included the noteworthy step of repackaging and redefining atheism as merely the lack of belief that a God or gods exist. This, supposedly, puts the atheist in the position of not asserting any truth claim and thus not needing to bring arguments for one. That is the theist's job.

But there are other atheist strategies being employed as well. While some are relatively new, others have been around for a while but persist with new twists and expressions. Most involve the claim that theism is either *rationally* or *morally* defective, or both, and therefore it is unfit for any right-thinking person. In the following two chapters, we will address both these claims.

Chapter 9

Strategy #3: Is Theism Morally Defective?

As noted above, there are other atheist strategies being employed as well, ones which are unrelated to questions of burden of proof, definitions of atheism, and the like. Most consist of claiming that when theism is put under the microscope, it is found to be either *rationally* or *morally* defective, or possibly both. Either way, it is not a live option for any clear-headed person. Why, exactly, would anyone assert that theism is morally defective?

GOD HAD OTHER OPTIONS SO WHY DIDN'T HE TAKE THEM?

One recent way of claiming that theism is morally defective consists of arguing that some of God's big actions, like his creation of the world and the creatures in it, were defective because he had other, better options at his fingertips which would have made life better for the creatures and, in some cases, saved them vast amounts of suffering. He did not choose these options when he surely could have. As one atheist professor has put it,

> Either God isn't smart enough to figure out how to create a good world, or he doesn't have the power to do it, or he

> just doesn't care. You pick. These are the logical options given this world.[1]

These are highly unappealing choices to say the least. Worse yet, they are all inconsistent with the character and attributes of the Judeo-Christian God who is totally good, all-powerful, and all-knowing.

A FEW EXAMPLES

What are some options God could supposedly have chosen, and the appalling results he could have avoided by choosing them? And what kind of case does this make against theism? A few examples will do.

Richard Carrier, American historian and critic of Christianity, sets out a number of options which would be available to any God who possessed the powers and moral goodness the Christian God is said to have:

> There are many things God could do. He could make all true bibles indestructible, unalterable, and self-translating. He could make miraculous healing or other supernatural powers so common an attribute of the virtuous believer that they would be scientifically studied and confirmed as surely as any other medicine or technology. Hospitals would even have *bona fide* "faith healing" wings. . . . He could speak to all of us in the same voice, saying the same things.[2]

Earlier in the same passage, Carrier becomes even more explicit about specific things he himself would do if he had the powers and moral goodness which the Christian God is said to have:

> I would immediately alleviate all needless suffering in the universe. All guns and bombs would turn to flowers. All garbage dumps would become gardens. There would be adequate resources for everyone. There would be no

1. Loftus, *Why I Became an Atheist*, 240.
2. Carrier, *Why I Am Not a Christian*, 19.

> more children conceived than the community and the environment could support. There would be no need of fatal or debilitating diseases or birth defects, no destructive Acts of God. And whenever men and women seemed near to violence, I would intervene and kindly endeavor to help them peacefully resolve their differences. That's what any loving person could so.[3]

As far as Carrier is concerned, the fact that God has not availed himself of these options is reason enough to conclude that the God of Christianity does not exist. It is worth reading his own words to this effect:

> Therefore, the fact that the Christian God does none of these things—in fact, nothing of any sort whatsoever—is proof positive that there is no Christian God.[4]

Another entirely different example of an option God had but did not take is given by John Loftus, philosopher and critic of Christianity. God could have created heaven right off, he argues, and avoided putting his creatures through the vast amount of illness, pain, and suffering they are experiencing in this world. Heaven is said to be a place free of sorrow, pain, and death. Why not simply start with it? Surely, God had the option of doing so but he did not take this option. He chose earth for us first and the result is dreadful suffering.[5]

One more example also from Loftus: God gave us free will even though he must have known we, as a human race, would misuse it in such appalling ways. He could have withheld it. What would we think of a father who handed his two-year-old child a razor blade to entertain himself, asks this critic? Furthermore, who would we blame if the child ended up with cuts on her fingers and arms? The questions continue. What would we think of a parent who warned his son not to swim in the deep end of the pool and

3. Carrier, *Why I Am Not a Christian*, 18–19.
4. Carrier, *Why I Am Not a Christian*, 20.
5. Loftus, *Why I Became an Atheist*, 236.

then sat by watching as the son chose to ignore the warning and drowned?[6]

Most of us would agree that it is unwise, and possibly immoral, to give something to someone knowing ahead of time they will tragically abuse it. It's a principle all good parents live by. If a child misuses a particular freedom, parents take it away at least for a while. Why then, asks this critic, would God give us the powerful gift of free will knowing we would use it to perpetrate such pain and suffering in this world? Why does God now stand by and watch as an intruder wipes out an entire sleeping family, or a serial rapist terrorizes and harms women for years on end?

Surely God had, and has, other options concerning human free will, and this critic has a few suggestions. For one, God could have handled free will for us on earth just as he plans to in heaven. Either people in heaven will have free will or they will not. If they will, it means that somehow there must be a way to have free will without sin and evil because heaven is a place free of such ills. On the other hand, if people will not have free will in heaven, it means it is possible to live meaningful lives without it. If so, then God could have withheld free will on earth, or limited its use, to prevent great evils. Even now he could go further and place different intentions in the minds of people planning evil or cause mechanical failures to prevent them from inflicting suffering on others or cause certain extremely vicious people to die at birth.

The point, say these critics and many others like them, is that we can all think of other things God could have done. Options should not be a problem for God so why not avail himself of them?[7]

DOES THIS LEAD TO ATHEISM?

The first thing to note about this line of reasoning is that if it is meant to be an attack upon God's existence, it misses the mark. If

6. Loftus, *Why I Became an Atheist*, 237.

7. Loftus, *Why I Became an Atheist*, 237.

God could have done things differently, then, at the very least, God must exist. Non-existent beings do not carry out actions of any kind. So as an argument for atheism, it is a nonstarter.

Still, it is a different kind of case against theism, and it is being made by atheists today. It is, at best, a challenge to a particular kind of God, namely one who is said to be morally good and also powerful enough to create the universe; in other words, a God like the God of Christianity. To understand the precise nature of this challenge, notice again the statement set out above by one who argues this way:

> Either God isn't smart enough to figure out how to create a good world, or he doesn't have the power to do it, or he just doesn't care. You pick. These are the logical options given this world.[8]

In other words, God's refusal to avail himself of other options, such as the ones suggested above, leaves us with three possibilities. It challenges either God's wisdom (he isn't smart enough), his power (he was not able to do things differently), or his goodness (he doesn't care about the suffering his choices have caused). These are the choices. When taken together, it all means that a God who is all-wise, all-powerful, and perfectly good does not exist. If he did, surely he would have chosen some of the better options available to him.

WHAT FOLLOWS?

Is it really true that God's failure to take the options mentioned above means he is not powerful or good or smart enough to choose them? American philosopher and former president of the American Philosophical Association, Alvin Plantinga, in writing about the larger problem of evil, sets out another possibility which is relevant to this discussion.

It is at least possible, he observes, that God has a good reason for what he does, even the things which are puzzling to us. We may

8. Loftus, *Why I Became an Atheist*, 240.

not know what God's reasons are, but that does not mean they do not exist. Notice how he applies this principle to the existence of suffering and evil in our world:

> Suppose that the theist admits he just doesn't know why God permits evil. What follows from that? Very little of interest. Why suppose that if God *does* have a good reason for permitting evil, the theist would be the first to know? Perhaps God has a good reason, but that reason is too complicated for us to understand. The fact that the theist doesn't know why God permits evil is, perhaps, an interesting fact about the theist, but by itself it shows little or nothing relevant to the rationality of belief in God.[9]

It's hard to deny Plantinga's point here, and we should apply it to the discussion at hand. It is at least possible that God had, and has, good reasons for not availing himself of the options suggested by the critics above, and this represents a fourth option. To rule this option out, we would need to know much more than any human knows. Of course, we may wish we knew what his reasons are, but, as Plantinga notes, nothing really follows from the fact that we do not. God still may have them just as any good parent has reasons for things they do to which their children are not privy. The upshot of this is that we are simply not forced to conclude that God is either not smart enough, not powerful enough, or just doesn't care. It may be that he is all of these things but has good reasons for creating us and our world the way he did.

Carrier seems to be aware of this response and attempts to rebut it in the following comment:

> A Christian can rightly claim he is unable to predict *exactly* what things his God would choose to do. But the Christian hypothesis still entails that God would *do something*. Therefore, the fact that God does *nothing* is a decisive refutation for the Christian hypothesis.[10]

9. Plantinga, *God, Freedom, and Evil*, 10.

10. Carrier, *Why I Am Not a Christian*, 20.

By doing something, Carrier presumably means God would intervene to stop bad things from happening at the times Carrier thinks he should. It is simply incorrect, however, to assert that Christianity entails that God would *do something* if that means to intervene and prevent every bad thing from happening. The Christian position is that God does intervene to stop certain bad things but not all of them, and he has good reasons for when, how, and if he chooses to intervene in any given situation. As Plantinga has said above, the fact that we may not know what God's reasons are does not mean he does not have them. Given this understanding, God's lack of intervention in a particular instance of evil is no refutation of Christianity.

IS THE FOURTH OPTION A COP-OUT?

Some may wonder if appealing to God's reasons is a cop-out, a handy way out of a dicey problem. Actually, it is a condition for anyone who accuses God, or anyone else for that matter, of committing an immoral, unjust, or cruel act. Good reasons for our actions change the nature of those actions. In many cases, they remove culpability altogether. They are the difference between a criminal who kidnaps and confines a neighbor, and the police who put the same criminal behind bars when they finally arrest him for his crime; or between a cruel sadist who pokes a baby with needles to watch her scream, and a doctor who gives the same baby an injection to protect her from future diseases. In each case, both actions look the same from the outside, but one is criminal abuse while the other serves justice, safety, and health. The difference rests entirely on the presence of a good reason for one action but not for the other.

CAN WE SUGGEST REASONS?

Can we say more? Can we suggest plausible reasons God may have had for not availing himself of the kinds of options suggested for him earlier? While it is not strictly necessary to suggest reasons in order to show God could have had them, some have been suggested and are worth briefly considering.

GOD COULD HAVE WITHHELD FREE WILL FROM US, SO WHY DIDN'T HE?

Recall the challenge raised earlier concerning our free will. God could have made us without it and thereby saved his creatures from a great amount of pain and suffering. Can we propose any good reasons God may have had for choosing to make us this way, with free will instead of without it, even while knowing humans would misuse it?

One possible reason is not hard to imagine. It's true that free will can be abused, sometimes with terrible results, but it also makes possible some of life's greatest goods, things like loving friendships, happiness, and even the ability to carry out good commendable actions. Thus, God would have had good reasons for making humans free. Actions carried out by robots, even seemingly good ones like going around the room with a plate of snacks for everyone present, are never commendable. Any words of thanks or commendation are reserved for the people behind the robot who provided the snacks and directed it to act this way. C. S. Lewis, in speaking of free will, noted that creatures without it would be like robots and are "hardly worth creating."[11]

This will not surprise us. We apply this principle every time we hold someone responsible for their actions or words. We neither praise nor blame someone if we think they were forced to do what they did.

11. Lewis, *Mere Christianity*, 52–54.

GOD COULD HAVE CREATED HEAVEN FIRST, SO WHY DIDN'T HE?

What about the question of why God did not create heaven first and skip all the pain and suffering in our earthly existences? Interestingly, certain Christian philosophers have suggested that perhaps the type of life God had in mind for heaven was intended to follow our earthly life which came first.[12] How so? Why must this earthly life come first? It's not difficult to imagine why. God, in Christian theology, is a personal being who loves, cares, and has desires. He created us also as persons with the hope of enjoying meaningful relationships with us for eternity. Here's the crunch: For this to happen, we, the created persons, must be given the opportunity to choose to come into relationship with God or to say no thanks. Here is another crunch: This choice must be uncoerced and made freely for it to be a genuine choice. For this to happen, other appealing choices must exist as well.

None of us need be told that genuine personal friendships exist only when people enter them by their own choices. The least hint of coercion will cause the other party to question the friendship and maybe even the motives of the so-called friend. In the case of our relationships with God, heaven is the life given to people who freely chose life with God on earth amidst an array of other choices and attractions.

TWO OBJECTIONS

Still, someone might object: "But wouldn't God know from the start who would join with him? Did an all-knowing God really have to put us through this earthly existence to find that out? If not, then why not skip earth and go straight to a heavenly existence with the people who would have joined up with him?"

Yes, God would know this information, but is this really the way a personal being would do it? Think of what this suggestion

12. Christian philosopher Norm Geisler argues for this notion along with Winfried Corduan in their *Philosophy of Religion*.

would mean for the created persons. On this approach, they were never consulted nor given a chance to decide whether to be a part of this arrangement. They were merely informed that they either would or would not have joined with God if given the opportunity, so there is no need to bother giving them the choice. That step can be bypassed. This is not how real friendships are developed, however, and most people I know would not tolerate this way of making friends.[13]

Someone else might object that many children have died at birth or before the age of accountability, while millions of others have died through miscarriage or been aborted. Most Christians believe these ones will be in heaven even though they've never been through life on earth. If so, does this not call into question the necessity of an earthly experience before a heavenly one?

Perhaps the more important question is this: Regardless of how strongly God desires that people be given the opportunity to choose or reject him on earth, what should a good and just God do with people who are robbed of this choice? People like this are special cases. They are unlike the rest of us because, while they have neither chosen nor rejected God, they have also committed no sin nor done anything worthy of God's judgment. So the question becomes this: On what basis would a just God judge people like this or send them to hell? Since they have committed no sin or evil, it seems wiser to believe this kind of God would welcome them into heaven while people in normal circumstances continue to have the opportunity to chose or reject him.[14]

GOD COULD HAVE MADE US DIFFERENT, SO WHY DIDN'T HE?

Recall that one of the options suggested by Carrier above was for God to turn all garbage dumps into beautiful gardens and all guns

13. This suggestion was made by Canadian theologian D. H. Lunn in a public lecture at Trinity Western University on March 21, 2013.

14. This response was stimulated through the result of personal email correspondence with Canadian theologian D. H. Lunn on March 18–19, 2025.

and bombs into flowers. This, of course, would require that God either prevent people who make garbage dumps, guns, or bombs from achieving their ends, or manipulate their intentions from the outset so they no longer want to build these items.

Let's assume God could do all of these. Can we think of any sensible reasons why he did not? C. S. Lewis may provide some help here. In writing about the larger problem of pain and suffering in the world, he raised the question of whether God should have made us and the world different to diminish the amount of suffering in it, and if so, exactly how. He probed more deeply and asked what, exactly, we would want God to have changed, and whether we have considered the implications for life on earth if he had made the changes we wish for? His own words on these questions are insightful:

> We can, perhaps, conceive of a world in which God corrected the results of this abuse of free will by His creatures at every moment: so that a wooden beam became soft as grass when it was used as a weapon, and the air refused to obey me if I attempted to set up in it the sound waves that carry lies or insults. But such a world would be one in which . . . freedom of the will would be void; nay, if the principle were carried out to its logical conclusion, evil thoughts would be impossible, for the cerebral matter which we use in thinking would refuse its task when we attempted to frame them. All matter in the neighbourhood of a wicked man would be liable to undergo unpredictable alterations. That God can and does, on occasions, modify the behavior of matter and produce what we call miracles, is part of the Christian faith; but the very conception of a common, and therefore, stable, world, demands that these occasions should be extremely rare. In a game of chess you can make certain arbitrary concessions to your opponent. . . . But if you conceded everything that at any moment happened to suit him . . . then you could not have a game at all. So it is with the life of souls in a world: fixed laws, consequences unfolding by causal necessity, the whole natural

> order, are at once . . . the sole condition under which any such life is possible.[15]

Let's apply Lewis's point in this passage to the question at hand. Let's imagine God responded to the critics by saying, "Yes, that's a good idea. Let's change this person's intentions so he no longer wants to produce a gun but a bouquet of carnations instead. There, it's done." Apart from any unintended side-effects this change might cause, it should, at least in theory, diminish the overall amount of pain on earth. But pain would still be abundant everywhere we turned. So now what, asks Lewis? Why not go further and step in anytime conflict is near and bring about a peaceful resolution? But there would still be a great deal of suffering. God could go further and cause all hard objects to turn into soft pillows just before coming down on people? Still there would be substantial evil and pain in our world. Perhaps God could change our cruel words into nice ones, or even our mean thoughts into generous ones. Would these changes satisfy? It's doubtful since there would still be a lot of pain and suffering in our world, more than we would want. My guess is that the critics would be right where they are now, questioning God for not taking further actions to diminish the suffering they still see around them. I see no end in sight apart from God eradicating pain in our world altogether. To do that, he would have to interfere in every human decision and action, and we would then be functional robots doing exactly what God decides we should do and with the effects he permits. What would be gone is the liberty required to live like persons and make decisions between real choices that matter. But if the life of real persons who make important choices was what God had in mind for us, then he will interfere in our thoughts, decisions, and actions only rarely in what we call miracles.

How much free will should we have and how often should God intervene? Only an omniscient being could answer that, and the answer will be in accord with his purposes in creating us in the first place.

15. Lewis, *Problem of Pain*, 33–34.

WHAT ABOUT HEAVEN?

There is, however, another harder hitting objection concerning free will. This one may be new to some, but is commonly raised by critics of theism and, in fact, was mentioned above. It can be stated simply: What about heaven? Will people there have free will? It's a simple-sounding question, but it may catch us off guard. There are two possible answers: yes or no. Suppose we answer, yes, people will have free will there. If so, then it means there is a way for us to be free and yet have no sin, suffering, or pain since heaven is a place free of these. This means human freedom does not necessarily have to entail the possibility of evil choices. Somehow it can exist amid a sinless, perfect situation. If that will happen in heaven, then God could have done it here, too, so why didn't he?

Suppose, however, we answer, no, there will not be free will in heaven. This would seem to indicate that one can live a happy fulfilled life as a person without human freedom. So why didn't God make earth a place where that happens? Either way, it seems like our present situation on earth is unnecessary.

One answer to this conundrum has been suggested by Canadian theologian D. H. Lunn, who draws a connection between earthly and heavenly life. If we choose to join with God on earth amid an array of other choices and temptations, says Lunn, then in heaven we will be rewarded with a new nature similar to Jesus' own nature. Anyone who has read the accounts of Jesus will know he was tempted during his earthly life and was free to respond as he wished, but doing evil was unthinkable for him and he remained without sin (Heb 4:15).

Lunn's suggestion is that God's gift to all who choose him on earth will be a nature like Jesus. We will be free to do evil but it will be out of the question for us.[16] This suggestion shows how it is possible for us to be free and sinless at the same time, but only with new natures given as part of our heavenly lives.

16. This suggestion is set out in an unpublished paper by Canadian theologian D. H. Lunn entitled "Will There Be Free Will in Heaven?"

Lunn's proposal is worth considering, especially since it accords with the New Testament's own description of the kind of nature Jesus' followers will receive in the future. The apostle John wrote that "when Christ appears, we shall be like him, for we shall see him as he is" (1 John 3:2). There will surely be much more to the transformation we go through, but, at the very least, this statement points to a fundamental change in which our characters become like that of Jesus.

Chapter 10

Strategy 4: Is Theism Rationally Defective?

If theism is not morally below par, the question still remains whether it is in trouble rationally. The charge that it is rationally defective will not be new to anyone who has engaged others recently on questions of faith, religion, and God. When one inquires as to how or where the irrationality lies, one finds a variety of answers. The bottom line, however, is that somehow, in some way, when theism is examined carefully, it fails the test of being rational, credible, or coherent. In short, it is something a clear-thinking person should not believe.

This is not a new critique. One of the best-known versions of it was argued in 1936 by the young English philosopher A. J. Ayer, who contended that the statement "God exists" is not simply false, it's worse. It is in such trouble, he said, that it is simply meaningless and does not even rise to the level of being either true or false. Hence it could be set aside with no further consideration. Ayer declared that the statement "There exists a transcendent god" has no literal significance.[1]

How could he make such a dramatic claim? He did so by establishing a verification criterion of meaningfulness according to which, for a statement to be meaningful (not true, just meaningful), it had to be either an *analytic truth* (a statement like 2 x 2 =

1. Ayer, *Language, Truth, and Logic*, 158.

4, which is true by virtue of the meanings of the words in it), or *empirically verifiable* (one which can be tested by observation, as scientists do). Since the statement "a transcendent God exists" does not satisfy either of these criteria, he declared it to be meaningless.[2]

At the time, his view caught on and spread widely, but as the noted atheist philosopher Graham Oppy has recently remarked, enthusiasm for Ayer's reasoning has "evaporated almost entirely" since the mid-twentieth century for a number of reasons.[3] Chief among them is the fact that when Ayer's verifiability criterion of meaningfulness was put under the microscope, it soon became evident that it failed its own test. The criterion itself was neither an analytic truth nor was it empirically verifiable as it demanded for any statement to be meaningful. In other words, the criterion did not meet its own requirements to be a meaningful statement. In the words of one of my philosophy professors, if Ayer's criterion is true, then it is meaningless.[4] Quite a mess! As Alvin Plantinga observes, Ayer's proposal, called Logical Positivism, "has retreated into the obscurity it so richly deserves."[5]

The strategy of labelling theism irrational, however, did not end with A. J. Ayer. Others have found new ways of making this charge. Graham Oppy has explained that the notion of a God with properties like omniscience, omnipotence, omnipresence, goodness, etc., like the Judeo-Christian God, is thought by some to involve logical inconsistencies.[6] What are these alleged logical inconsistencies, and how exactly do they work?

2. Ayer, *Language, Truth, and Logic*, 52.

3. Oppy, "Arguments for Atheism," 58–59.

4. This description of Ayer's criterion of meaningfulness was made by Professor Michael Wreen in a philosophy class at Marquette University in 1987, wherein I was a student.

5. Plantinga, *Warranted Christian Belief*, 8.

6. Oppy, "Arguments For Atheism," 59–61.

ONE EXAMPLE: THE PROPERTY OF OMNIPOTENCE

The concept of omnipotence (the notion that God is all-powerful), is one commonly raised example of an attribute of God which has been called self-contradictory.[7] If the notion of omnipotence is a logically contradictory property, then it could not exist as a real property in the same way a square circle could not exist in the real world. This means, of course, that no being could have this property. There could be no such thing as an omnipotent being, something the Christian God is said to be.

How, exactly, is omnipotence said to be logically inconsistent or incoherent? There are a number of ways but perhaps two will do for our purposes. One common way, sometimes referred to as the paradox of the stone, is to ask if God is able to create a rock so big he cannot lift it. Only two answers are available. He either *can* or *cannot* create this rock, and the alleged problem is that both answers involve something God cannot do. Furthermore, the problem is said to arise precisely because of the concept of omnipotence. This property is what is supposedly generating this logical contradiction. A non-omnipotent being, like any of us, could quite easily build an object that it could not lift: a chunk of cement, shed in the back yard, tree house, etc. The logical problem arises only once the notion of omnipotence enters the picture.

Does the concept of omnipotence truly generate logical contradictions? Does the paradox of the stone really prove omnipotence is irrational, or is there a way to resolve this paradox and still believe in an omnipotent God?

A Closer Look at the Paradox of the Stone

So can God create a stone so big he cannot lift it? If he *can* create this stone, then there is something he cannot do—lift it. On the other hand, if he *cannot* create this stone, then again there is something he cannot do—create it. Either way, it seems we are faced with the reality that there is at least one thing an omnipotent

7. Oppy, "Arguments for Atheism," 59–61.

God cannot do. Does this threaten the coherence of the concept of omnipotence and thus of an omnipotent God?

C. Wade Savage, American philosopher of science, argues that it does not and has suggested an interesting response to show why. He suggests that we simply answer no to the question. No, God is not able to build a rock so big he cannot lift it. In giving this answer, it may sound like we have limited God's power, but have we? By saying God is not able to create rocks that he cannot lift, we have said that God's power to *create* rocks is limited by his power to *lift* them, says Savage. He can create only rocks that he can lift. Again, this sounds like a limitation on God's power to create until we realize that God's power to lift is infinite; he can *lift* any rock of any size. Notice what follows from this. If his power to *create* rocks is limited only by his power to *lift* rocks which is infinite, it follows that he can also *create* any rock of any size. It turns out that this "limitation" of God's power ends up placing no restriction whatsoever on God's power to create.

Savage's answer is reminiscent of the answer often given to the question of whether God can create a square circle. Since the words "square circle" do not refer to any actual thing, there could be no such thing as a square circle. For this reason, it is generally recognized that even an omnipotent being could not make one. This represents no reduction in the power of an omnipotent being, but rather a recognition that the words "square circle" are mere gibberish and do not refer to anything. Omnipotence means the power to do anything that can be done, not the ability to do things that *cannot* be done, like creating square circles. As C. S. Lewis says,

> It remains true that all things are possible with God: the intrinsic impossibilities are not *things* but nonentities. It is no more possible for God than for the weakest of his creatures to carry out both of two mutually exclusive alternatives; not because His power meets an obstacle, but because nonsense remains nonsense even when we talk it about God.[8]

8. Lewis, *Problem of Pain*, 18.

How does this apply to the question of whether God could create a rock so big he could not lift it? Since an omnipotent being could lift any rock, it means there is no such thing as *a rock an omnipotent being could not lift*. No such rock could exist and therefore these words fall into the same category as the words *square circle*. They, too, are gibberish. Since omnipotence refers to the power to do anything that can be done, not things that cannot, it means that even an omnipotent God could not make such a rock since none could exist. Again, this represents no reduction in God's power.

To summarize, according to Savage, when theists hear the question "Can God make a rock so big he cannot lift it?," they should answer, "No, he cannot because there is no such thing as a rock God cannot lift. He can build any rock and lift any rock."[9] It turns out that answering no to this question involves no diminishing of God's power whatsoever. It simply clarifies what omnipotence would mean in this situation. Furthermore, rather than calling into question the rationality of the concept of omnipotence, it turns out to be a clever question that simply requires us to define this concept with greater precision.

Is There a Conflict Between God's Omnipotence and His Moral Goodness?

Another alleged problem with the property of omnipotence consists in claiming that it conflicts with some other essential property God is said to have. One example, explained by Graham Oppy, is to claim that omnipotence is incompatible with goodness. No being could be both omnipotent and perfectly good at the same time.[10] Why not? Because a perfectly good being would want a world without evil (or else what does it mean to be good), and an omnipotent being should be able to create such a world. Obviously, our world is full of evil, pain, suffering, and other things which are

9. Savage, "Paradox of the Stone," 74–79.

10. Oppy, "Arguments for Atheism," 59–61.

not good. How could this be if God were both omnipotent and morally good?[11]

Much analysis has been done on the relation between the attributes of goodness and omnipotence. Perhaps the most succinct reply to it is the one given by Alvin Plantinga, mentioned above when replying to the atheist's complaint that God could have availed himself of other better options in creating us and the world. There, we noted Alvin Plantinga's response was that it is always possible that a morally good God does exist and has good reasons for making us and our world the way he did. From the fact that we may not know what his reasons are, it does not follow that there are no reasons. His statement is worth reading again for its relevance to our present question concerning the alleged conflict between God's goodness and omnipotence:

> Suppose the theist admits he just doesn't know why God permits evil. What follows from that? Very little of interest. Why suppose that if God *does* have a good reason for permitting evil, the theist would be the first to know? Perhaps God has a good reason, but that reason is too complicated for us to understand. The fact that the theist doesn't know why God permits evil is, perhaps, an interesting fact about the theist, but by itself it shows little or nothing relevant to the rationality of belief in God.[12]

Plantinga's insight here is that it is possible that there is a God who has morally sufficient reasons for allowing evil in our world. As long as this possibility remains, no conflict can be shown between his moral goodness and omnipotence.

In the end, Graham Oppy himself does not find these kinds of attacks on the coherence of God's properties convincing because the reasoning always depends upon particular definitions of the properties. Other definitions are always available which escape the charge of being irrational, incoherent, or inconsistent with some other of God's properties.[13]

11. Oppy, "Arguments for Atheism," 59–61.
12. Plantinga, *God, Freedom, and Evil*, 10.
13. Oppy, "Arguments for Atheism," 59–61.

Chapter 11

Strategy #5: Does Theism Breed Violence?

In the previous two chapters, we examined the charge by some atheists that belief in a God who is all-knowing, all-powerful, and good, is undermined because, upon closer examination, this concept of God is found to be either morally or rationally defective, or possibly both.

A fifth, and related, strategy is employed by certain atheists who allege that theism, the belief in God, is dangerous. It supposedly breeds violence, intolerance, and the willingness to carry out unthinkable atrocities. While this charge is not new, it has been developed and argued passionately over the past two decades, and has received the label "new atheism." It has caught the public imagination and changed the conversation regarding God, faith, and religion in the Western world so we must take it seriously.

How, exactly, is religion said to be dangerous? Religion, say the new atheists, with its belief in God, has a power unmatched in this world to motivate people to carry out atrocities. Words like "God" and "Allah" must go the way of "Apollo" and "Baal" lest they destroy us all. As Sam Harris, a prominent advocate of this strategy, puts it, this belief is leading people to kill others, and the fact that young people around the world are being educated in fundamentalist religious schools should terrify us.[1]

1. Harris, *End of Faith*, 133.

Harris expresses the situation more fully in the following dramatic words:

> Believe that you are a member of a chosen people . . . in . . . an evil culture that is turning your children away from God, believe that you will be rewarded with an eternity of unimaginable delights by dealing death to these infidels—and flying a plane into a building is scarcely more than a matter of being asked to do it.[2]

Richard Dawkins, British biologist and another prominent new atheist, explains what makes this belief, and the people who hold it, so dangerous. People like this, he says,

> know they are right because they have read the truth in a holy book and they know, in advance, that nothing will budge them from their belief. . . . The book is true, and if the evidence seems to contradict it, it is the evidence that must be thrown out, not the book.[3]

Let's be clear that, according to the new atheists, the problem is not the people themselves. It is the power of religion and the belief in God to turn good people into bad and to move them to carry out atrocious actions which would be unthinkable to them if not for this belief. Here is how Richard Dawkins describes the people themselves:

> However misguided we may think them, they are motivated . . . by what they perceive to be righteousness, faithfully pursuing what their religion tells them. They are not psychotic; they are religious idealists who, by their own lights, are rational.[4]

New atheists sometimes go a step further yet and call into question the moral nature of God as well as certain religious doctrines. God is described by Richard Dawkins as "arguably the most unpleasant character in all fiction: jealous and proud of it; a petty,

2. Harris, *End of Faith*, 44.
3. Dawkins, *God Delusion*, 282–85.
4. Dawkins, *God Delusion*, 304.

unjust, unforgiving control-freak; a vindictive, bloodthirsty ethnic cleanser; a misogynistic, homophobic, racist, infanticidal, genocidal . . . malevolent bully."[5]

THREE QUESTIONS

How can we respond to these hard-hitting charges? Do new atheists have a point? Is there a kernel of truth in their charges against religion? People do commit atrocities because they believe their God commanded them to, don't they? New atheism has been addressed more fully elsewhere, so our responses here can be concise.[6] Three questions should be asked to assess the new atheist charges.

Question 1: Does This Strategy Prove Atheism?

The first thing to note about this strategy is that, as an argument for atheism, it does not get far. In other words, even if new atheism's claims concerning the dangers of religion and belief in God turned out to be true, it still would not prove there is no God. The arguments brought forward by new atheists do not show, or even try to show as far as I can tell, that God does not exist, but only that the belief in God is destructive and, therefore, we should not hold it or, at the very least, not act on it. It is a different kind of case against theism.

Question 2: If Religion Were Eliminated, Would the Violence Stop?

This question is a critical one since this new atheist strategy depends upon a yes answer to it. If religion is, indeed, the cause of violence, destruction, intolerance, as new atheists contend, then it

5. Dawkins, *God Delusion*, 31.

6. For a fuller explanation and critique of new atheism, see Chamberlain, *Why People Don't Believe;* McGrath and McGrath, *Dawkins Delusion.*

would follow that if religion were removed from the world, the so-called religious violence, intolerance, etc., would end. But would it? Unfortunately for new atheism, there are a number of reasons to think the answer is no, that the elimination of religion would not stop the so-called religious destructive behavior.

Violence Is Inflicted by Both Religious and Nonreligious People

First, shocking violence has been perpetrated throughout the history of the world by both religious and nonreligious people. In fact, when one looks at the human record of human violence, one is led to wonder if the amount of violence and persecution inflicted upon religious people by nonreligious perpetrators is greater than so-called religious violence. One organization which tracks such activity is International Christian Concern, an international nonprofit group with a mission of giving hope to persecuted Christians around the world. Its website describes the current situation this way:

> Christians are sitting in prison simply because of their faith. Many corrupt governments and discriminatory legal systems target religious beliefs, incriminating people for believing in, sharing, or converting to the Christian faith.[7]

Another is Open Doors. In 2025 it reported that more than 380 million Christians around the world are suffering persecution for their faith, with 310 million suffering high or extreme levels.[8]

Lest we think bloody persecution of religious believers is a thing of the past and the world has now moved beyond such evils, the following story, reported by Open Doors on February 18, 2025, will disabuse anyone of that notion. It describes events which took place less than two weeks before the story appeared. The title tells it all: "70 Christians Found Beheaded in Church in DRC." DRC is

7. Persecution.org, "Write Letters."
8. Open Doors, "World Watch List 2025."

the Democratic Republic of Congo, a country in which Christians have experienced increased persecution in recent years. Here is the story as reported by this organization:

> According to field sources, at around 4am last Thursday (13 February) suspected militants from the Allied Democratic Forces (ADF)—a group with ties to so-called Islamic State (IS)—approached homes in Mayba in the territory of Lubero, saying: "Get out, get out and don't make any noise." Twenty Christian men and women came out and were captured.
>
> Shaken by this incident, people from the local community in Mayba later gathered to work out how to release those held captive. However, ADF militants surrounded the village and captured a further 50 believers. All 70 of those kidnapped were taken to a Protestant church in Kasanga where they were tragically killed.
>
> Muhindo Musunzi, director of the Kombo primary school [which belongs to the CECA20 church], says that prior to this incident, churches, schools and health centres had all shut their doors because of the chaotic security situation. "We had to move all activities towards Vunying," he said.
>
> Field sources report that, until yesterday (Tuesday 18 February), some families had not been able to bury their dead because of insecurity in the area. Many Christians have now fled the area for their safety.
>
> "We don't know what to do or how to pray; we've had enough of massacres," says an elder of the CECA20 church. "May God's will alone be done."[9]

Examples of religious believers being persecuted for their faith are easy to come by. Nor is this a new phenomenon. Paul Marshall, a Canadian professor who has researched this history, has reported that in the years following the Bolshevik Revolution in Russia, the violence inflicted upon religious believers of all kinds was shocking. Government officials developed techniques of tyranny and when the believers tried to resist, they were often thrown in prison, tortured, or worse.

9. Open Doors, "Christians Found Killed."

Marshall has noted that in the 1920s and 1930s alone, "Approximately two hundred thousand Russian Orthodox priests, monks, and nuns were slaughtered. A further half million were imprisoned or deported to Siberia." Soviet authorities systematically destroyed the vast majority of churches and priests during the period between 1918 and 1941. A Russian state commission which investigated these practices later described the horrific treatment of religious leaders this way in 1995:

> Most priests were shot or hanged, although other methods used by Communist death squads included crucifying pastors on their church doors [or] leaving them to freeze to death after being stripped and soaked in water during winter.[10]

In China, the violence inflicted upon religious believers in pursuit of an atheist agenda was even worse. Chairman Mao's reign from 1949 to 1976 was filled with brutal campaigns and resulted in literally millions of deaths.[11] Marshall observes that Communism was held to be supreme, and religion was seen as a threat. Here is how he describes the appalling violence done against religious people during this period:

> In the Cultural Revolution from 1966 to 1976, probably tens of millions of people were killed and tens of millions more disgraced. In this period, the Red Guards were particularly brutal with China's believers, whether Christian, Muslim, or Buddhist. It was perhaps the largest intense persecution of Christians in history. The level of atrocity that took place during that epoch is beyond comprehension.[12]

Perhaps we wonder, was this violence really motivated by an anti-religious agenda, or could the real motives behind the violence have been different? Even if so, the fact would remain that a vast amount of violence has been inflicted on religious people

10. Marshall, *Their Blood Cries Out*, 121–22.
11. Marshall, *Religious Freedom in the World*, 99–101.
12. Marshall, *Their Blood Cries Out*, 75–79.

by people with no religious affiliation. Furthermore, to see that Chairman Mao's motivation was, indeed, an anti-religious agenda, it is important to understand his actual strategy. Religious believers were instructed to accept Communism as supreme over their own faith. If they declined, they were labeled as "counter-revolutionaries" and sentenced to twenty years or more in prison or labor camps. From 1955 on, especially clergy were arrested, given long prison terms, and also treated viciously in China's "reeducation through labor" camps. In the 1960s and 1970s, Mao stepped it up and closed all places of worship in his efforts to crush religion altogether.[13]

The facts are unmistakable. A great amount of violence has been inflicted upon religious believers by nonreligious perpetrators. In fact, as noted above, the violence carried out against religious believers may well surpass that ever done in the name of religion.

We should not miss the significance of this. It means that the hope of eliminating, or reducing, violence by eliminating religion from the world is a false one. The more one examines the overall situation, the clearer it becomes that neither religion nor the lack of it, is the real cause of the violence. Cruelty is inflicted in great amounts by perpetrators, religious or not. It appears that the true cause lies elsewhere.

The True Causes Lie Elsewhere

The second reason to doubt that if religion were eliminated the so-called "religious violence" would cease, or even be seriously reduced, is provided by Robert Pape, professor of political science at the University of Chicago and a specialist in international security affairs. Given the avalanche of media stories highlighting the religious beliefs of perpetrators of certain highly publicized acts of terror, it is no wonder so many of us simply take it for granted that the cause of the violence is religion. Professor Pape challenges this

13. Marshall, *Their Blood Cries Out*, 75–79.

notion. He has spent a career analyzing causes and motivations of individual acts of terrorism throughout the world and argues that to lay the blame at the feet of religion, as much of the media tends to do, is not only simplistic, but overlooks other critical facts.

In one study, he analyzed the causes and motives behind every suicide bombing from 1980 to 2005. His conclusion was that we are too hasty if we think religious motivations are all there is to it. Acts of terror such as suicide attacks that look, at first glance, like religious violence often have deeper political motivations. Religious belief, he says, is neither necessary nor sufficient to move people to carry out suicide attacks. In other words, these attacks may occur with no religious motivation at all, and even when religion does play a role, it is never enough, by itself, to cause the suicide bomber to attack. The deeper motivation is usually political, not religious, and it would remain regardless of whether religion played any role. Readers will not be surprised to hear that in many cases, the real reason behind the attack is the desire to force an occupying nation to get out of one's homeland by people who lack sufficient military might to go to war with the occupying force.

Pape adds that this political motivation is sometimes linked with religion and sometimes it is not. When it is, religion becomes a useful instrument to move people to willingly give their lives in a violent act. The crucial point, contends Pape, is that these violent actions would happen with or without religion's involvement.[14]

One other question concerning new atheism should be asked. This one pertains specifically to Christian believers but it is a question for anyone attempting to identify the true cause of the so-called religious violence.

Question 3: Do Jesus' Teachings Lead to Violence?

The question is this: If people fully followed the teachings of Jesus, would they be led to commit acts of violence? Let us admit that

14. See Pape, *Dying to Win*, for a fuller explanation of the political motivations behind suicide attacks. See also Gambetta, *Making Sense of Suicide Missions*.

some Christians throughout history have inflicted violence upon others. There is no point in trying to deny this fact. The question here is a different one, namely, if people truly followed the teachings of Jesus, would they be led to violent actions? This question is important since the new atheist charge is that religion, including Christianity, breeds violence and is toxic for our world.

Even a brief look at Jesus' teaching, however, reveals that the more closely we follow it, the more we will respect human dignity and equality, and the more we will promote peace and act generously toward others. It's not a stretch to say that if everyone followed Jesus' teachings, our world would be a joyful and peaceful place. A brief look at a few of his teachings will suffice.

The Golden Rule

Perhaps the most well-known of Jesus' teachings around the world is what has come to be called The Golden Rule: "Do to others what you would have them do to you" (Matt 7:12). It is hard to think of a more effective rule of thumb for our dealings with others. Treat others as we would wish to be treated by them. It is simple to understand and easy to apply. Furthermore, few things can clarify our moral obligations in any situation more quickly than a reflection on this rule. Simply put the shoe on the other foot and ask how you would want to be treated if the situation were the other way round.

Interestingly, Jesus set out no program for how to apply this rule in individual situations. Such a program would not be practical. It's a principle meant for all times and situations, and we all must apply it in our own circumstances.

The Call to Love People of All Kinds

Many people are aware that Jesus emphasized to his followers the importance of loving others around us. In fact, he called it the second greatest commandment, second only to the call to love God himself (Matt 22:37–40). The theme of loving others and doing good to them was a constant in Jesus' teachings. God is deeply pleased, he said, when people feed the hungry, show hospitality, clothe people who need clothes, visit prisoners, console those who are grieving, and help the sick (Matt 25:31–46). He promised dire consequences for those who do not.

There is more to Jesus' teaching on this issue, however. He extended the call to love others in two surprising ways. First, he called us to love not just our friends but our enemies too (Matt 5:44). Secondly, he called us to love people who are not part of our social groups. Nowhere did he teach this more powerfully than in the well-known parable of the Good Samaritan (Luke 10:30–37). In the story, after others had avoided a wounded traveler who had been viciously attacked by bandits, a Samaritan stopped to assist him, applying oil to his wounds, bandaging him up, transporting him to a local clinic, and paying for his treatment. This story has special force when we remember that, in first-century Palestine, the Samaritans and Jewish people had an ongoing hostility toward each other so intense that they both avoided each other's territory. And yet, in Jesus' story, the Samaritan looked beyond this hostility, saw a person in need, and stopped to show kindness.

Furthermore, Jesus lived out this teaching throughout his ministry. He spent time with "sinners," prostitutes, and tax collectors, groups which were marginalized and thought to be unclean in his culture. To the dismay of the religious leaders of his day, Jesus went to their homes, visited with them, and shared meals. He also paid the price for it. One of the primary charges made against him by the religious elite of his day was that he welcomed and touched such people.[15]

The bottom line is that, while the followers of Jesus have not always lived up to his teaching, anyone who follows it consistently will not be led to acts of violence. We would do well to reflect daily on these words of Jesus which capture the essence of what it means to follow him:

15. Matt 8:3; 9:20–25; 21:31–32; Luke 15:1–2.

> But I tell you, love your enemies and pray for those who persecute you, that you may be children of your Father in heaven. . . . If you love those who love you, what reward will you get? Are not even the tax collectors doing that? And if you greet only your own people, what are you doing more than others? Do not even pagans do that? (Matt 5:44–47)

Jesus Taught Human Dignity and Equality

The teachings of Jesus mentioned above all make sense when we realize that, as someone who endorsed the Old Testament, Jesus also believed humans are inherently valuable. Furthermore, this dignity and value does not stem from our abilities, race, social standing, contributions to society, or any other features or qualities we may have. We have dignity and value simply because we are human, or more specifically, because we are purposeful creations of God who made us "in his image" (Gen 1:26–27). This is a foundational truth for followers of Jesus, and it underlies, and makes sense of, all his other teachings.

It does something more. If human dignity stems from our creation by God, and thus from our humanness, then it follows that *all* people have *equal* worth and dignity because we all are humans and have all been created by God in his image. This provides an unshakable foundation for the principle of human equality. While this principle is often abused, it is hard to think of a more important one for how we all treat others. It is the basis for Jesus' other teachings mentioned above: love of all including one's enemies and those from outside groups, justice for all, and the Golden Rule. These teachings flow naturally from the principles of inherent human dignity and equality. In them, they have a solid rationale and make perfect sense.

We have been examining strategies employed by atheists for making their case, but perhaps we need to back up a step and ask why we should think there is a God in the first place. Can we just assume theism and go from there? As we noted earlier, it is probably wisest to assume neither theism nor atheism to be the default position. Both views make important truth claims, and thus, both need supporting reasons.

It is not uncommon to hear atheists state that they find the arguments or evidence for God to be implausible, unconvincing, or unsuccessful. These are very easy statements to make, but they technically express only the states of mind of the ones who make them. They tell us little about the strength of the arguments or evidence itself. Some atheists go even further and either state or imply that there is no evidence whatsoever for God's existence or any other Christian teaching. It simply does not exist. Sam Harris, American new atheist, writes that the beliefs of Christianity, including belief in God, "float entirely free of reason or evidence."[16]

So let's ask, can we prove God exists? How would one go about doing such a thing? Are there convincing reasons to believe this important claim? It is to these questions that we now turn.

16. Harris, *End of Faith*, 17.

PART 2

Signs Pointing to God

Chapter 12

Can God Be Proven?

THE QUESTION OF WHETHER God can be proven is one I have put to students over the years and the responses have varied greatly. A few blurt out, "No, of course not!" Others do not feel comfortable going this far, but are not sure they can say yes either. Of course, a wide group usually hold their fire, unsure of what to say.

Our answer to this question, as in many other important ones, hinges on the meaning of the word "prove." If we are asking whether we can prove God's existence with logical certainty, then not many people will answer yes. Nor is this considered to be a serious problem since few, if any, of our beliefs about the real world can be proven in this way. Philosophers enjoy showing how the most obvious, and seemingly certain, of our beliefs can be doubted and thus must be held with less than 100 percent certainty. As an exercise, try to think of something, anything, you currently think or believe for which no possible doubt could be brought, such as the fact that you are in the room you are in right now reading these pages. Bertrand Russell's "brain-in-the-vat" example is commonly raised to show that there is at least some basis for doubting even beliefs like this one.[1] In other words, logical certainty about the real world is an elusive gem.

1. For a full volume dedicated to various analyses and implications of the brain-in-a-vat example, see Goldbert, *Brain in a Vat*.

We accept most of our beliefs, even our important ones, for reasons which, to us at least, seem adequate bases for them. Those reasons could involve our own personal investigation into the matter or, as in most cases, the acceptance of the word of others we trust. And our level of conviction is proportional to the strength of the supporting reasons but seldom do we reach the level of logical certainty.

So perhaps the better question is to ask whether there are strong reasons for believing God exists. Are there signs pointing to God's existence which are convincing enough to justify one's belief in God? Philosophers, scientists, and others have suggested some, and we will examine a few of them shortly. First, a brief comment should be made about the special challenge facing anyone desiring to prove the opposite claim, namely, that there is no God.

ATHEISM'S BUILT-IN CATCH

I asked my students one day what they would need to do to prove the statement "There are no golf balls in this room." Easy, just look through the room, they replied. When I asked how much of the room they would need to examine, they all agreed they could not miss any part of it since, if they did, the golf ball could be in the part where they did not look. I then extended the area to our university campus, and asked what it would take to prove there are no golf balls in this university. They began to chuckle knowing what they would need to do: check every square inch of the campus, which in our case is a sprawling one. I then changed the statement to this: "There are no golf balls in China." Immediately one front-row student spoke up with a profound response: "You're screwed!" he said. It was a fun moment in class. I especially liked this response because it showed the student caught the point, so I pressed one step further. Imagine the statement we were trying to prove was this one: "There are no golf balls in or out of the universe." By that time, the point was made, and many of them threw up their hands.

My last statement was what logic textbooks call a universal negative, and it is parallel with the atheist claim "there is no God in or out of the universe." As we noted earlier in this book, C. S. Lewis pointed out that atheism involves the claim that back behind the things science observes, there is no supernatural divine being.[2] The atheist claim, if we state it in full form, is the following: "There is no God anywhere in or out of the universe."

Notice two features of this claim. First, it is not a scientific claim since it concerns what lies behind the things science observes. If we are to answer it at all, we will need to look beyond science's normal methods of inquiry. Secondly, as was noted above, this claim is not merely a negative one, it is a *universal negative*. It claims not merely that God does not exist here or there, but anywhere, in or out of the universe. As such, it presents a serious difficulty for anyone wanting to show it is true. *Simple negative* claims abound and are often easy to prove or disprove. Here are a few: there are no camels in this room; it is not raining outside; there are no boats in the lake this morning. *Universal negative* claims, however, are a different matter since they claim much more. In fact, they claim something well beyond the reach of us humans. It would require omniscience to know that no God exists anywhere in or out of the universe. This should, at the very least, make us open to the idea of God's existence even before checking into the evidence either way.

As noted above, a number of Christian philosophers and theologians have contended not only that God exists, but that he has left signs of his presence for all to see. In the following chapters, we'll briefly examine six of these signs.

2. Lewis, *Mere Christianity*, 22.

Chapter 13

Six Signs Pointing to God

ARE THERE SIGNS POINTING to God? According to C. S. Lewis, they are all around us. Here is how he described his own inability to miss the signs as a young atheist:

> In reading Chesterton, as in reading MacDonald, I did not know what I was letting myself in for. A young man who wishes to remain a sound Atheist cannot be too careful of his reading. There are traps everywhere—"Bibles laid open, millions of surprises," as Herbert says, "fine nets and stratagems." God is, if I may say it, very unscrupulous.[1]

A number of prominent Christian philosophers and theologians continue to think God has left signs of himself throughout the universe, and in this chapter we will put forward six of these signs. Readers are invited to consider how clear and compelling they find each one, especially in the light of the difficulty of supporting atheism seen above.

SIGN ONE: HUMAN DNA POINTS TO GOD

Imagine taking a stroll along your favorite beach, perhaps enjoying some fish and chips. Suddenly, you see carved in the sand right where you are walking your name, both first and last, along with

1. Lewis, *Surprised by Joy*, 181.

the word "welcome." There it is, a brief message written in the sand welcoming you to the beach.

What would you think? You could wonder if the wind blew the sand in just such a way that these word shapes appeared. There are lots of other little ruts and grooves in the sand which were put there by the wind or water washing over them. The shapes formed by the elements would have to end up some way so why not in words welcoming you to the beach? But if it was your name, along with a welcome greeting, you would find it difficult to believe this is how those shapes came to be. There is something different about them than all those others. What is the difference? It is that these shapes contain ideas, information.

Notice these words by John Lennox, professor of mathematics and philosophy of science at Oxford University, concerning the significance of finding information not just in the sand but elsewhere in our world as well:

> We have only to see a few letters of the alphabet spelling our name in the sand to recognize at once the work of an intelligent agent. How much more likely, then, is the existence of an intelligent Creator behind human DNA, the colossal biological database that contains no fewer than 3.5 billion letters, the longest "word" yet discovered?[2]

Regardless of our level of understanding of human DNA, genetics, or the human genome, Lennox's point is not hard to grasp. It raises an intriguing question: Could a basic understanding of human DNA reveal it to be a pointer to God? Lennox answers with an enthusiastic yes. Like the words at the beach, the existence of human DNA, he says, likewise contains information and thus points to an intelligent creator behind it in a far greater way than a few words written in the sand. Where there is information, there is intelligence behind it.

Go back to the beach for a moment and ask yourself again how you might immediately react upon seeing your name written in the sand with a welcome. I, for one, would stop short and

2. Lennox, *God and Stephen Hawking*, 74.

immediately begin looking around for someone who wrote those words—a friend or family member who knew I would be there that day and was watching nearby to enjoy my surprised reaction. The fact that I did not know who wrote the words would not stop me from thinking someone did. The human genome, says Lennox, also contains information—3.5 billion letters worth.

Lennox, of course, is not alone in drawing out this implication of human DNA. Dr. Francis Collins, one of the world's most prominent scientists and a widely recognized expert on human DNA, has drawn out the same implication in great detail in a book entitled *The Language of God: A Scientist Presents Evidence for Belief.* Collins was the director of the National Institutes of Health in the United States for twelve years and prior to that led the Human Genome Project culminating in 2003. This endeavor mapped out and revealed the human DNA sequence for the first time in history and allowed us to understand our own genetic structure in a way we never had before. Through this process, he and his team discovered the genes associated with a number of diseases to the great benefit of the world. He refers to the human genome as "this most remarkable of all texts," and describes his experience of being involved in the sequencing of this text as "both a stunning scientific achievement and an occasion of worship."[3]

Collins is also a Christian, and his way of bringing together the meaning of God's existence and the practice of science should stand as a clarion call and provide a pattern for scientists and nonscientists alike, so many of whom in our current culture are struggling with how to relate these two important areas of thought. Collins directs two important questions to such people:

> Will we turn our backs on science because it is perceived as a threat to God, abandoning all the promise of advancing our understanding of nature and applying that to the alleviation of suffering and betterment of humankind? Alternatively, will we turn our backs on faith,

3. Collins, *Language of God*, 3.

> concluding that science has rendered the spiritual life no longer necessary?[4]

Notice his answer to both options:

> Both of these choices are profoundly dangerous. Both deny truth. Both will diminish the nobility of humankind. Both will be devastating to our future. And both are unnecessary. The God of the Bible is also the God of the genome. He can be worshipped in the cathedral or in the laboratory. His creation is majestic, awesome, intricate and beautiful and it cannot be at war with itself. Only we imperfect humans can start such battles. And only we can end them.[5]

Collins and Lennox are pointing out that human DNA, which scientists now understand far more fully than just a few decades ago, is a majestic text containing information in its 3.5 billion letters. Information points to a mind behind it, and it is no different with the information contained in this astounding text. As such, it is a sign pointing to a cosmic "writer" of this text. If we look for someone who wrote a few words in the sand, then how can we not look for someone who stands behind the human genome? This leads to our next sign, also put forward by John Lennox.

SIGN TWO: MINDS POINT TO GOD

Perhaps we have never thought of human intelligence or consciousness as pointers to God but consider these words, also from John Lennox:

> Either human intelligence ultimately owes its origin to mindless matter, or there is a Creator. It is strange that some people claim that it is their intelligence that leads them to prefer the first to the second.[6]

4. Collins, *Language of God*, 211.
5. Collins, *Language of God*, 211.
6. Lennox, *God's Undertaker*, 210.

It is important to understand Lennox's point in this intriguing statement. He is addressing the question of how a special kind of thing came to be, namely, things which think, believe, and doubt—in other words, minds.

It's one thing to ask how things in general came into being, why anything exists rather than nothing, and different answers have been given to that question. But asking where minds and consciousness come from pushes this question to a new level. Even if we think we can answer the question of how things in general came to be, the existence of minds and consciousness still need to be explained. Lennox's pointed question is: Can a mind be produced by mindless matter? If the answer is no, then it calls for an intelligent creator.

Interestingly, the atheist philosopher Thomas Nagel has raised the same question and, in fact, has written an entire fascinating book entitled *Mind and Cosmos*, which calls into question the ability of a purely materialistic evolutionary account (one which does not include God) to explain the existence of minds and consciousness. In his book, Nagel refers to the current widely accepted view as "physico-chemical reductionism" or "evolutionary naturalism" and argues that this approach which is so widely held today is unable to explain a number of key features in our world related to minds, including intentionality, meaning, value, and, more specifically, "conscious thinking creatures." He goes to great lengths to set out what an adequate explanation of mind and consciousness would need to explain and spends chapters arguing that evolutionary naturalism comes nowhere close to being able to provide such an explanation. In his view, this is a major problem for the current way of understanding the world since minds and consciousness are such prominent entities in our world. He asserts this as an atheist himself, one who is in search of a better explanation for the existence of minds and consciousness in the cosmos.[7]

Nagel's contention here is the same as the one made by John Lennox above. These two thinkers, one an atheist and the other a theist, are in agreement. They diverge only when they go further

7. Nagel, *Mind and Cosmos*, 5–8, 13–20, 23.

and search for what could adequately account for mind and consciousness in our world. Nagel notes that while God would provide an explanation, he as an atheist is not satisfied with theism and would prefer to keep searching for an alternative non-theistic explanation.

Lennox sees no such need. He happily asserts that human intelligence and the ability to think and reason are far better explained by a cosmic mind which created them than by pure mindless matter. In fact, he contends that the more one knows about human intelligence, the stronger it points to an intelligent creator behind it. This leads to our next sign which points to a different, and fascinating, phenomenon which also calls out for explanation.

SIGN THREE: THE RELIABILITY OF OUR COGNITIVE FACULTIES POINTS TO GOD

Imagine the following conversation by a second–year philosophy student named Jane and her mother Sue:

JANE. Mom, do you think the things you believe are true?

SUE (*Pausing.*) Now there's a new one. I've never been asked that before. What things?

JANE. Everything you believe—your big beliefs and your small ones. Your beliefs about things like morality, God, the meaning of life, and about what you had for breakfast this morning or that your car needs an oil change soon.

SUE. (*Slightly shaking her head.*) You're asking if I think my beliefs are true?

JANE. Yes.

SUE. (*Pausing*) Well, I guess I could be wrong on some of them, but if I didn't think they were true, I wouldn't believe them, would I? Isn't that what it means to believe something? You at least *think* it's true.

Jane. Good point. So then do you also think the reasoning processes in your brain, your cognitive faculties which produce all your beliefs, can be relied upon to produce beliefs which are true most of the time?

Sue. Whoa! Where is this coming from?

Jane. My philosophy course. Our professor wanted to know if we thought our thinking processes were reliable most of the time. He called them our cognitive faculties which produce our beliefs.

Sue. Well, if this is a survey, my answer would be the same. I can't see any good reason *not* to rely on . . . what did you call them again?

Jane. Your cognitive faculties.

Sue. Who knows, maybe they have a few bad days like the rest of us and go off track once in a while, but even then, I think I can usually figure that out and correct them eventually. I guess that means I'm assuming my cognitive faculties are basically reliable.

Jane. You actually said that more clearly than my philosophy professor. Have you considered a career change?

If most of us were asked whether we thought our beliefs were true or whether we could trust our cognitive reasoning processes to produce true beliefs most of the time, we would probably give the same answer as Sue. There is virtually a universal conviction among us that our well-considered beliefs are usually true; otherwise, we wouldn't believe them. In other words, we normally feel we can rely on our cognitive faculties, our minds, memories, and perceptions to give us reliable information about the world outside us most of the time. So what?

Could it be that this widely held conviction is itself a pointer to an intelligent creator of our minds and cognitive processes? A number of highly regarded philosophers have thought so. Alvin Plantinga and C. S. Lewis before him have both put forward fascinating reasons to believe that if we do indeed trust our cognitive faculties to give us reliable information about the world outside us, as we all do, then we have a strong reason for believing there is an intelligent creator behind our minds and thinking faculties. In other words, our confidence in our cognitive faculties points to an intelligent creator behind them. How does this work?

Let's take C. S. Lewis first. In his book entitled *Miracles*, he drew attention to something most of us recognize implicitly, namely, that there is more than one way we hold our beliefs. One way is to hold them because we have what Lewis calls *proofs* for them. These would be logical grounds, evidence, data, etc., which provide a basis for thinking a belief is true. But there is another way some of our beliefs arise. Some of them are the result of *nonrational causes*. For example, certain ideas may seem right, in fact obvious, to us because of our nationality, family background, religious affiliation, etc. Lewis notes that if a particular belief you or I hold is produced by nonrational causes, we would hold that belief whether it was true or not. This means that telling someone their belief can be explained by nonrational causes is a quick and dirty way to discredit the belief. Furthermore, we all seem to know this instinctively. Notice how Lewis put it:

> The most popular way of discrediting a person's opinions is to explain to them casually—"You say that *because* (Cause and Effect) you are a capitalist, or a hypochondriac, or a mere man."[8]

Lewis's point here is that when we tell someone they are holding a particular belief for reasons like these, we are attributing that belief to something other than rational causes such as evidence or logical grounds, and it often elicits the following reaction: "Sure I'm a capitalist or . . . but that's not the only reason I believe this. I believe it because . . ." The speaker then normally proceeds to provide a *proof* or logical ground for their belief, something different than a nonrational cause. In other words, both parties seem to agree that if the belief really were brought about strictly

8. Lewis, *Miracles*, 26–28.

by nonrational causes, it would be discredited. Lewis seems to be right when he adds,

> The implication is that if [nonrational] causes fully account for a belief, then, since causes work inevitably, the belief would have had to arise whether it had grounds or not. We need not, it is felt, consider grounds for something which can be fully explained without them.[9]

In other words, if a belief can be fully explained by nonrational causes, then the person would hold it whether it is true or not. It's a striking point, but one that is not hard to understand.

Lewis, then, raises a remarkable question by asking whether it might be possible that most, or all, of our beliefs could be explained this way, namely, by nonrational causes. If so, it would mean that, contrary to what most of us assume, we have little reason for trusting most of our beliefs as true. How could this be possible? What nonrational causes?[10]

Lewis's answer is that the view called naturalism explains all our beliefs by nonrational causes. Naturalism is the view that there is no God; nature is all there is. Furthermore, every physical event is caused by a preceding physical event. Once the cause is in place, the effect, or event, will follow inevitably. Since our brains are purely material entities, they too operate this way. The neurons firing in my brain, causing my beliefs, only do so as they are caused to fire this way by other preceding physical causes. The implications of this view for the truth of our beliefs are dramatic. Lewis himself sets them out by quoting Professor J. B. S. Haldane, a contemporary of his who was a renowned biochemist, geneticist, and science writer. Haldane wrote the following words:

> If my mental processes are determined wholly by the motions of atoms in my brain, I have no reason to suppose that my beliefs are true . . . and hence I have no reason for supposing my brain to be composed of atoms.[11]

9. Lewis, *Miracles*, 26–28.

10. Lewis, "Religion Without Dogma?," 170.

11. Haldane, *Possible Worlds*, 209.

This concise statement has enormous implications for the way we think about our beliefs. Professor Haldane was claiming that however strongly we may feel our beliefs are true or that we hold them for good rational reasons, the fact is that if they are purely the results of physical processes, the movement of atoms in my brain, then I have little reason for trusting them to give me the truth. The beliefs would be what they are whether they were true or not since nonrational causes, the movement of atoms in my brain, have produced them. Most interestingly, he adds, this applies to all our beliefs, including the belief that one's brain is composed of atoms which determine our mental processes. This way of thinking about how our beliefs come to be ends up discounting itself. It turns out to be a self-refuting belief. If you believe it, you will need to conclude there is no reason to think it is true.

Contemporary American philosopher Alvin Plantinga has caused a stir within the philosophical world by taking this idea further. He notes that if naturalism is true, then not only are our beliefs the result of purely physical nonrational processes as described by C. S. Lewis, but the evolutionary process which has brought us to this point has itself not been aimed at producing *truth* in the first place. Rather it is aimed at enhancing our *fitness for survival and reproduction*. But if so, says Plantinga, it raises the question of whether we have reason to trust our beliefs as true. His answer is that there simply is no need for them to be *true* so long as they enhance our fitness for survival. They may be true but whether they are or not does not really matter. What matters is that they enhance our chances for survival, not that they be true. It would be nice if they were true, and some of them may be, but their truth cannot be counted on. Their main aim is to contribute to our fitness for survival and reproduction.

So what are the chances, he wonders, that any particular belief we hold is true? He puts it at approximately fifty-fifty. It might be true, but there is an equal chance this belief would turn out to be false. If so, then comes a second question: If it is fifty-fifty, then what is the likelihood that our cognitive faculties which produce our beliefs are reliable? It must be very low, he answers. If your belief-producing mechanism constantly produces beliefs which have as much chance of being false as true, you will not trust it as reliable. The upshot is that, on naturalism and atheistic evolution, we have little reason to trust the cognitive faculties which produce our beliefs to be reliable. Our beliefs could be right; they could be wrong. We have a fifty-fifty chance.[12]

As we noted earlier, however, we all do think our beliefs are true most of the time, i.e., that our cognitive faculties and belief-producing mechanisms are reliable, that we can count on them to give us fairly accurate pictures of the world around us. We live by this assumption, and it forms the basis of all of our reasoning. If we did not assume it, ironically we could not even hold views like naturalism or atheism as all naturalists and atheists do. We're all in the same boat, relying on our cognitive faculties to produce true beliefs most of the time and being confident that they do.

This means, however, that if we assume our cognitive faculties *are* reliable and produce true beliefs most of the time, as we all do, we have a powerful reason to reject naturalistic evolution, i.e., to reject the notion that our cognitive processes are purely the result of naturalistic physical processes which are aimed at survival and reproduction.

Fortunately, there is an alternative to naturalism which does provide a solid basis for our confidence in our reasoning processes, and it is the point of this entire discussion. It is the view that our reasoning capacities have been given to us by an intelligent creator and are aimed at producing true beliefs. On this view, their purpose from the get-go is to produce true beliefs so it makes sense to assume, as we all do, that we can trust them to do so most of the time. In other words, the assumption we all have that our belief-producing cognitive processes can be relied upon to produce true beliefs most of the time is a sign pointing to an intelligent creator behind them. This creator gave us our cognitive faculties and made them in such a way that they are aimed at producing truth.

12. Plantinga, *Where the Conflict Really Lies*, 344–45. Also, see Plantinga's interview with Robert Lawrence Kuhn: Templeton Prize, "Evolutionary Argument Against Naturalism."

Again, it is not surprising that some have questioned Plantinga's view that naturalist evolution undercuts our confidence in our cognitive faculties to produce true beliefs most of the time. One challenge, perhaps the most common one, can be put simply: Wouldn't beliefs that promote our survival need to be true? Don't truth and correct information about the world contribute to our survival? In other words, aren't people with accurate information about the environment in which they live better positioned to adapt and survive in it than those who have false impressions of it? If so, it would not be correct to say, as Plantinga does, that a naturalistic evolutionary process has no concern with truth but only survival. The concern with survival would lead to a concern with truth. If so, our widely held confidence in the reliability of our beliefs makes perfect sense if naturalistic evolution is true.[13]

It's a thoughtful objection, and Plantinga has replied to it in a number of ways. First, he asks why we should think that true beliefs contribute to our survival. There certainly is no guarantee of that, he contends. Beliefs could contribute to our survival without being true. In fact, we can imagine all kinds of ways that false beliefs would promote our survival at least as well as true ones, maybe better at times. When a grizzly bear approaches you in the woods, it doesn't really matter whether you think it is dangerous and liable to harm you, or that it is warm and friendly like Smokey the Bear and wants to come give you a big hug, something you and everyone you know detests. You simply are not into being hugged by bears. Either belief will cause you to turn and get out of there and thus will enhance your chances of survival.

Plantinga's point is that, however strongly we may value truth, that is simply not what evolutionary naturalism is aimed at. It is aimed at our survival, and we can trust it for that, but there simply is no basis for trusting it to give us truth. It might and might not since it is aimed at survival, not truth.[14]

13. Plantinga, *Where the Conflict Really Lies*, 344–45. Also, see Plantinga's interview with Robert Lawrence Kuhn: Templeton Prize, "Evolutionary Argument Against Naturalism."

14. Templeton Prize, "Evolutionary Argument Against Naturalism."

Plantinga adds a different type of response to this question as well. We may want to argue in any number of ways, he notes, that our reasoning processes are reliable. Few of us can stand the thought that they are not. The objection stated here concerning the need for our beliefs to be true is one such argument. There is, however, a deep problem in arguing for the reliability of our reason, he notes. The moment we begin making the argument, setting out premises and inferring conclusions, etc., we are already using our reasoning processes. In fact, we are already assuming our reason is reliable, the very thing we are trying to prove. Simply put, we cannot *prove* the reliability of reason without already *using* reason and assuming in advance that it is reliable. If, however, our reasoning processes are the result of the motions of atoms in our brains and part of a naturalistic evolutionary process aimed at survival, not truth, then we have no basis for trusting anything we supposedly prove by using reason. If, on the other hand, they were given to us by an intelligent creator who aimed them at producing truth, our assumption that they are reliable makes perfect sense.[15]

It appears we've come full circle. We all assume we can trust our reasoning capacities and rely on them to produce true beliefs most of the time. It's our starting point and way of getting along in the world. From there, we carry on all our reasoning *on the basis of* this assumption. What we may not have realized is that this widespread assumption points to an intelligent creator who gave us our belief-producing mechanisms and designed them for producing the true beliefs we all assume they deliver.

SIGN FOUR: OUR MORAL CONVICTIONS POINT TO GOD

Few questions are more foundational for the way we think about morality, the meaning of life, where we came from, or what happens when we die than whether there is something behind our universe. Most people around the world believe there is, but there have always been some who disagree.

15. Templeton Prize, "Evolutionary Argument Against Naturalism."

Quarreling and a Transcendent Moral Law

C. S. Lewis pursued this question vigorously, but surprisingly, when he did, he did not actually start with it. The question he began with was whether a transcendental moral law exists, something he called a *Law of Human Nature.* If so, he reasoned, then we need to consider what kind of being, if any, lay behind *it*. But how does one go about figuring out whether such a transcendental moral law exists? There are many ways of approaching this question, and Lewis's approach is as unusual as it is fascinating.

He began with the phenomenon of human quarrelling. We've all heard it and, unfortunately, done it. None of us are strangers to it. It can be humorous to watch, or awkward or unpleasant, but can we learn anything from the way people quarrel? Most of us have probably never dissected a good quarrelling match to see exactly what is being said or assumed by people as they quarrel, but that is what Lewis asked his readers to do. He believed the way we quarrel reveals something important in our deeper thoughts, and it relates to the question of whether a transcendental moral law exists in our universe.

How does this work? Lewis noted that when we humans argue with each other, we do not merely fight like cats and dogs—shouting, kicking, or scratching—at least not most of the time, thank goodness! We say things like "How'd you like it if anyone did the same to you?" or "That's my seat, I was there first" or "Leave him alone, he isn't doing you any harm" or maybe "Come on, you promised." In all these statements, and many others like them, Lewis noted we are appealing to a standard which we expect the other person already to know about and abide by. And in most cases, the other person's reply to us indicates that they do indeed know about the standard and wish very strongly to show they are not violating it. Notice how Lewis drew the connection between quarrelling and this moral standard:

> Now what interests me about all these remarks is that the man who makes them is not merely saying that the other man's behaviour does not happen to please him. He is

> appealing to some kind of standard of behaviour which he expects the other man to know about. And the other man very seldom replies: "To hell with your standard." Nearly always he tries to make out that what he has been doing does not really go against the standard, or that if it does there is some special excuse . . . some special reason in this particular case why the person who took the seat first should not keep it . . . or that something has turned up which lets him off keeping his promise.[16]

And what, exactly, is the significance of both parties trying to show their actions did not violate this standard of behavior? Lewis drew it out in the following words:

> It looks, in fact, very much as if both parties had in mind some kind of law or Rule of fair play or decent behaviour or morality or whatever you like to call it, about which they really agreed. And they have. If they had not, they might, of course, fight like animals, but they could not quarrel in the human sense of the word. Quarrelling means trying to show that the other man is in the wrong. And there would be no sense in trying to do that unless you and he had some sort of agreement as to what Right and Wrong are; just as there would be no sense in saying that a footballer had committed a foul unless there was some agreement about the rules of football.[17]

Lewis's point is quite clear. The way we argue with each other points to a law or standard which is known by us all. It's a law to which we hold others, and to which we will go to great lengths to show we have not violated. It really is true that there is no point in trying to show that another person is in the wrong unless you both had some agreement on what right and wrong are. This, of course, leads to the deeper question of how or why such a law exists. Is there something behind it?

Of course, we could avoid the whole question by treating this moral standard as if it were not real, merely a figment of our

16. Lewis, *Mere Christianity*, 17.

17. Lewis, *Mere Christianity*, 17–18.

imagination. As Lewis has shown, however, very few of us do treat it this way. We all feel the force of this moral standard pressing in on us, as a sense of obligation to do things like helping others even when we know we will receive nothing in return. Furthermore, most of us go to great lengths to convince ourselves, and others, that our actions somehow conform to this law. What we may not notice is that when we do this, we are demonstrating how seriously we take the moral law. We are treating it as though it is not only real but also correct. We do not want to be on the wrong side of it. But if this moral law exists, said Lewis, it cries out for an explanation. There must be something behind it which means, of course, that there must be something behind our universe. Lewis noted a couple of things we can say about the being behind the universe. Here is how he put it:

> What is behind the universe is more like a mind than it is like anything else we know. That is to say, it is conscious, and has purposes, and prefers one thing to another.[18]

Lewis's contention was that two things must be true of the being behind the universe. First, whatever it is, it looks more like a mind than matter since it obviously prefers some things over others, and secondly, the being behind the universe is extremely interested in right conduct. As he put it, the moral law which emanates from this being is as tough as nails.

Counterarguments

Does This Mean Atheists Have No Morality?

One of the most common objections raised concerning the Moral Argument comes in the form of a question: If morality comes from God or the Bible, then where do people who do not believe in God or recognize the Bible get their morality? Indeed, how could they have any moral concepts at all? Anyone who employs the Moral Argument in discussion will hear this question soon and often.

18. Lewis, *Mere Christianity*, 32.

The force of this objection rests in the fact that many atheists and non-Christians appear to live exemplary moral lives, often putting to shame those who claim to be Christians. If so, there must be something wrong with this alleged connection between God and morality.

Professor John Lennox recently responded to this question in a public forum by a university student who spoke for many in the audience.[19] Unfortunately, the question is based on a confusion of what exactly the Moral Argument asserts, and this, once again, highlights the necessity of stating such argument with accuracy and precision as Lennox proceeded to do.

This objection implies that if morality has its source in God or the Bible, then those who do not believe in God or read the Bible must have no access to it. This, however, is not an accurate understanding of either the Moral Argument or of Christian theology. As Lennox clarified, while the Bible sets out moral precepts, it is the nature of God, and not the Bible, that is the ultimate source of morality. God is a moral being who created all human beings in his image and infused them with moral knowledge whether they recognize God's existence or not. We speak of this moral knowledge in different ways, including having a moral conscience, moral concepts, or moral intuitions. This means all human beings have access to moral knowledge since all have been created by God and given a moral conscience.

Not only is this perfectly evident in our interactions with others but even the Bible itself notes that, at times, people who do not follow the God of the Bible demonstrate higher levels of both moral knowledge and conduct than those who profess to follow this God.[20] While this does not reflect well on the self-proclaimed

19. This question and John Lennox's response to it can be viewed at Naga Seminarian, "John Lennox Wisely Responds."

20. See Rom 2:14–15 where Paul reminds his audience of Christians that people outside the Christian community demonstrate both a knowledge of God's moral law and a willingness to follow it since it is written on their hearts. His words are these: "Indeed, when Gentiles, who do not have the law, do by nature things required by the law, they are a law for themselves, even though they do not have the law. They show that the requirements of the law

followers of God, it poses no problem for the Moral Argument for God which acknowledges that God has infused moral concepts in the minds of all people. It is this moral knowledge and sense of moral obligation, known and experienced by all people, that call out for an explanation.

Instinct and the Moral Law

Perhaps you're wondering if Lewis made too much out of this. Couldn't this all be nothing more than moral instincts like our other instincts? Lewis himself, however, clarified that our sense that we *ought* to act in certain ways is a different thing from our instincts. An instinct is simply a strong desire to do something whether it be a sexual instinct, fear instinct, or another, while the moral law tells us what we *ought* to do whether we desire it or not. Sometimes, our instincts should be acted on, but at other times they need to be restrained. In fact, added Lewis, the moral law often steps in to tell us which instincts we ought to follow and which should be momentarily suppressed.

Do Moral Codes Differ?

A different objection often raised against the idea of a transcendental moral law is derived from the existence of different moral codes around the world. In the minds of some, Lewis is simply mistaken to speak of one moral standard known to all people. This challenge has been raised emphatically by American anthropologist Ruth Benedict, who argued that moral values are much like clothing styles and rules of etiquette. They differ from culture to culture and even from time to time within the same cultures. To demonstrate her contention, she pointed to moral views on such things as slavery, homosexuality, the eating of cattle, ways of showing anger or joy, and even different views regarding the taking

---

are written on their hearts, their consciences also bearing witness, and their thoughts sometimes accusing them and at other times even defending them."

of human life, whether it be the lives of people from neighboring countries or even spouses, children, or parents. Suicide, too, she contended is viewed differently. From this she concluded that moral norms are culturally defined. There is no unified standard as Lewis contended.[21]

This objection is well known, and Lewis, who understood it well, was not persuaded by it. The real striking thing about the various moral codes around the world, he contended, was not how different they are from each other but rather how strikingly similar they are, especially given the other many differences in cultural practices, histories, and life circumstances. We can find some differences in moral practices, he acknowledged, but if we examine them carefully, we will find the same law running through them all. To see this, he said, we should consider what a truly different moral value would look like. Imagine a person receiving a medal for running away in battle, being praised for selfish actions, or rewarded for ignoring the needs of others. Or we could try to imagine a society in which political candidates got elected by bragging about the number of people they had deceived or cheated, the promises they'd broken, or the items they'd stolen. These would reflect truly different moral values, and finding such moral codes will prove difficult.

To demonstrate the deep similarity in moral codes, Lewis compiled a set of moral codes from the ancient Egyptians, Jews, Babylonians, Hindus, and Chinese to highlight the fundamental similarities between them. In all of these codes, there are moral imperatives against murder or cruel treatment of other human beings. There are also commands to honor and respect parents, elders, and ancestors. Furthermore, honesty, mercy, and care for children are commended.[22]

21. Benedict, "Defense of Moral Relativism," 45. For a fuller and more contemporary explanation of cultural relativism, including more on Ruth Benedict's position, consult Wolff, *Introduction to Moral Philosophy*, 21–39. For a higher level academic discussion of cultural relativism, see Tilley, "Cultural Relativism."

22. Lewis, *Abolition of Man*, 95–121.

We can also point to the Universal Declaration of Human Rights, a document written in 1948 and signed by over one hundred nations as another indication of the fundamental similarity in value systems around the world. It is a remarkably specific document in which human freedom, dignity, life, liberty, security, and a host of other values are labelled as morally good. Racial and gender discrimination, slavery, arbitrary arrest, torture, and all forms of degrading treatment are condemned.[23] This is not to say that everyone who signed the document lives up to its demands. In fact, none of us live up even to our own personal moral codes completely, but we still acknowledge the moral code as setting out good and bad conduct.

This, of course, does not mean there are not exceptions. We all allow for behavior which we would normally condemn in highly specified situations. In our society, we approve of spying on others' private activities in wartime. We send police informants into dangerous gangs to build friendships and earn trust in order to gain information for the express purpose of double-crossing the one whose trust has been gained. Other societies have their own similar exceptions.

Even here, however, we do not believe that actions like spying or double-crossing are morally good in themselves. We give them temporary qualified approval only when they are seen as the only way to avoid greater evils. We approve of them in unusual circumstances when not doing so would lead to an even worse situation, such as a military victory by a tyrant, and we place tight restrictions around their use.

MORAL PRACTICES VERSUS MORAL VALUES

Many others have replied to this challenge raised by Ruth Benedict as well. American philosopher Francis Beckwith has noted that the fact that people disagree about something, including moral values,

23. The Universal Declaration of Human Rights is included in UNIFO Staff, *International Human Rights Instruments*, 57, 117. It is also recorded in the appendix of Ashmore, *Building a Moral System*, 163–66.

does not show there is no truth in the matter. People have disagreed about many things, including the shape of the earth, the position of the earth among the planets, or whether we should treat people equally. Just as in these cases, the existence of different moral values does not automatically show there are no correct moral values. It takes more to show that, especially given the widely held assumption that a transcendent moral standard exists as evidenced in the way humans quarrel.

Furthermore, Beckwith and others have argued that different moral *practices* found in various cultures do not necessarily even reflect different moral *values* in the first place. Rather, different *practices* may be due to differences in peoples' *circumstances in life* or even their *beliefs about some aspect of reality.*[24] When we see a practice which seems radically different than ours, says Beckwith, we must ask *why* people are doing it. It is not enough simply to observe that they are engaging in this practice.[25]

Philosopher James Rachels agrees and points to the Eskimo's former practice of infanticide primarily on female babies as an example. When this practice was first discovered, it sent shock waves through the Western world and seemed to show that the Eskimos held a radically different value of human life than we do. It also appeared to show that cultural relativism was correct and that there was no transcendent moral standard as Lewis contended. Notice how things change, however, when Rachels asks the question of *why* they carried out these practices:

> But suppose we ask *why* the Eskimos do this. The explanation is not that they have less affection for their children or less respect for human life. An Eskimo family will always protect its babies if conditions permit. But they live in a harsh environment, where food is often in short supply. . . . Infant girls are . . . disposed of because, first, in this society the males are the primary food providers . . . and it is obviously important to maintain a sufficient number of food gatherers. But there is an important

24. Beckwith, "Critique of Moral Relativism," 14.

25. Beckwith, "Critique of Moral Relativism," 14–15.

> second reason as well. Because the hunters suffer a high casualty rate, the adult men who die prematurely far outnumber the women who die early.[26]

Rachels's point is that things look different when we go behind the actions and ask *why* this group treated their children in these ways. He draws his own conclusion about what this means for their moral values in these words:

> So among the Eskimos, infanticide does not signal a fundamentally different attitude toward children. Instead, it is a recognition that drastic measures are sometimes needed to ensure the family's survival. Even then, however, killing the baby is not the first option considered. Adoption is common; childless couples are especially happy to take a more fertile couple's "surplus." Killing is only the last resort . . . the raw data of the anthropologists can be misleading; it can make the differences in values between cultures appear greater than they are. The Eskimo's values are not all that different from our values. It is only that life forces upon them choices that we do not have to make.[27]

This example does not demonstrate that the Eskimos' actions were morally right, but it does show that different moral *practices* may not reflect different moral *values* at all once we examine why the actions are carried out.

The same principle applies to the highly contentious debate over abortion in Western society. It is commonly thought that two groups with the labels pro-choice and pro-life hold thoroughly different moral values. Although these two groups want different things, it simply is not the case that the moral values they hold are radically different from each other. Both groups believe human persons have a fundamental right to life. The pro-choice group, however, does not extend this right to fetuses because they argue they are not human persons. This argumentative strategy is very telling. Furthermore, both groups believe a woman should have

26. Rachels, "Critique of Ethical Relativism," 322–23.

27. Rachels, "Critique of Ethical Relativism," 322–23.

a right to do as she wishes with her own body, but pro-life people do not believe the growing unborn human inside a woman is part of her body. In addition, while pro-life people emphasize life, and pro-choice advocates emphasize liberty, both groups believe in both of these rights. In other words, it is too simple to claim the debate over abortion, as it is carried out, reflects radically conflicting value systems.[28]

Moral Progress and Moral Reformers

Two final reasons should be mentioned for accepting an objective moral standard. The first concerns the concept of moral progress. The very notion implies the existence of an objective, agreed-upon moral norm since without one there could be no moral progress. Moral progress means a culture is getting better, making progress, over time. Moral regress indicates it is getting worse, going downhill morally. The only way either of these could happen is if there is a moral norm, independent from any culture, to which a culture's practices are either drawing closer or more distant. If the morality of Martin Luther King Jr. is genuinely better than Nazi morality, it means there is an independent moral standard and Martin Luther King's morality is more in accord with it. If developments like the abolition of slavery, the enactment of civil rights legislation in the United States, and the banning of the practice of burning women at the funerals of their dead husbands truly represents moral progress, then there is an independent standard. If no such standard exists, such developments simply represent change, neither for the better nor the worse.

Nor could there be any moral reformers such as Mahatma Gandhi, William Wilberforce, Martin Luther King Jr., or General William Booth. If morality is measured only by the moral codes of individual societies (i.e., if there is no independent moral norm), then these reformers are actually acting immorally by violating those societal moral codes. If there is such a thing as moral

28. For a fuller explanation of the reasoning involved in the current abortion debate, see Beckwith, "Critique of Moral Relativism," 15–16.

progress and moral reformers to advocate for it, then an independent moral standard must exist.

The Concept of Tolerance

The second reason involves the much-discussed concept of tolerance. The need for tolerance in our world, and people's commitment to it, are often cited as important reasons for rejecting such a standard and supporting cultural relativism instead. To advocate a single objective moral standard is said by some to be intolerant of other groups which have different moral codes.

What is overlooked, however, is that the commitment to tolerance itself implies the existence of at least one universal objective moral norm, namely, tolerance. If it is true that we *ought* to be tolerant, this duty only makes sense if there is an independent objective moral standard according to which tolerance is morally superior to intolerance. So the commitment to tolerance itself is one more indication of the transcendent moral standard of which C. S. Lewis spoke.

SIGN FIVE: OUR FINELY TUNED UNIVERSE POINTS TO GOD

A number of years ago, I took part in a public meeting where young people were invited to ask any question they had about Christianity. It was an opportunity to hear what people were thinking and take our best shot at answering their questions. I and a professor of science were on the platform.

Audience members asked about the plight of people who had never heard of Jesus, about evil and suffering in the world, and other issues one might have expected. Then a group of students rose and identified themselves as students of my colleague, the science professor. Their question was blunt: "As a science professor, do you really think there is any evidence for God?"

To their obvious surprise, he answered without hesitation: "Yes, I do."

"What evidence?" they pushed.

He looked around for a minute and then pointed to a simple three-legged stool nearby. "This stool," he said, "has three legs, a flat seat made of solid material, and all positioned in such a way that it can be sat upon. It was obviously put together this way by someone who acted with intention." Then, looking up directly at his students, he drew the connection. "Your blood system," he said, "is far more complex than this stool, and yet the principle is the same. It functions in a way that allows blood to circulate through your body and give you life. It points toward an intelligent source far stronger than this stool does."[29]

This scientist was giving a simple version of what has traditionally been called the Design Argument. The argument from design has been around for centuries and thus has had many defenders and detractors over the years. American philosopher Robin Collins has developed sophisticated forms of this argument in recent times and is a helpful source for those wanting to learn about up-to-date, thoughtful discussions concerning it.[30]

Perhaps the most recent and interesting take on this argument builds on what scientists have come to call the fine-tuning of our universe. Fine-tuning refers to the notion that when the big bang occurred a long time ago and the universe came into being, it did not simply produce a blob of unorganized material. On the contrary, the big bang produced a universe which was specifically conducive to human existence. Scientists have discovered that the existence of intelligent life on earth depends upon a complex and delicate balance of initial conditions given in the big bang.

29. This conversation took place at an event called "Challenges to Christianity" hosted by Pastor Mike Penninga at Willow Park Church in Kelowna, British Columbia, in 2009.

30. Robin Collins is the distinguished professor of philosophy of science at Messiah University in Mechanicsburg, Pennsylvania, and is widely recognized for his numerous articles and lectures incorporating new scientific developments into the argument from design.

Of course, one might expect Christian scientists to talk this way, but here is how a leading scientist who is an unabashed atheist explains the fine-tuning of the universe. It remains one of the clearest and most compelling explanations I have ever heard. Leonard Susskind is the Felix Bloch Professor of Physics at Stanford University. The author of *The Cosmic Landscape: String Theory and the Illusion of Intelligent Design*, he is one of the pioneers of string theory. In a telling interview on the question of fine-tuning, he said,

> The laws of physics and cosmology, of how the universe evolved, are very special, and special in a way that is unexpected, in a way that seems to be very very conducive to our own existence.... These laws could have been different. For example, you could imagine a world that did not have electrons in it. There would be nothing wrong with that in basic mathematical theory of physics. Just throw away the electron. But if you did, there would be no atoms, no chemistry, no biology, no people to be here to ask the question.[31]

He then added another example. Gravity, he said, could be stronger. "It is very very weak, virtually negligible." When asked why gravity is so much weaker than the other forces, Susskind's answer was thought-provoking:

> We don't know but we do know that if it were even a tiny bit stronger, stars would burn out too quickly for life to evolve, and instead of stars and galaxies, we would have black holes because the universe would most likely expand and contract too rapidly and would burn out. We can't live in black holes, except in science fiction. Everything seems to be almost on a knife-edge.[32]

He summarized by declaring that if you were to change the laws of physics even a little bit, or the mass of this or that particle, or the temperature of the universe which is at a very narrow range

31. Closer to Truth, "Leonard Susskind."
32. Closer to Truth, "Leonard Susskind."

making it possible for liquid water to exist, or a couple dozen other "cosmic constants," then the world as we know it would not exist.

There is one cosmic constant about which Professor Susskind was particularly enthused, namely the cosmological constant. This one, he argued, is really on a knife-edge such that, in his words, "If it was to be changed by the tiniest tiniest bit, we would not be here."

What is the cosmological constant? It's a kind of anti-gravity, a repulsive force (as opposed to an attractive force), one that pushes out rather than pulls in. It's here in the universe, but what Professor Susskind found so stunning was that this force is infinitesimally small, far smaller than the mathematical calculations tell us it should be. The result is that it takes an enormously large space or volume for it to create any repulsive force at all. Why is this so? It is not because the mathematical equations tell us it must be this small, said Susskind. Quite the contrary. "It is this tiny," he said with a chuckle, "because whoever, or whatever, made the universe made it with an incredibly small cosmological constant." He noted the odds scientists have agreed upon of this force being what it is as 10 to the power of 123. "Nobody really knows why," he said again. What we do know, he added, is that if it were very much stronger, it would have blasted apart the galaxies, prevented stars from forming, and, in the end, prevented our existence.[33]

To summarize Professor Susskind, scientists have never understood why this force is so small but science tells us two things:

1. The cosmological constant is infinitesimally and unexpectedly small.
2. If it were not this small, there would be no life on the universe.

Professor Susskind is not alone in recognizing the fine-tuning of the universe. The existence of fine-tuning is widely acknowledged and discussed in the scientific community and the question which emerges from it is how it can best be explained. Unsurprisingly, there is some controversy over this question with

33. Closer to Truth, "Leonard Susskind."

some pointing to sheer chance, an option that Susskind ruled out. Others posit the possible existence of a vast and diverse multiverse. The reasoning is that if there were a large number of universes, then perhaps it is reasonable to suppose that at least one of them contains the conditions necessary for life to exist.

Apart from the fact that there is no independent evidence for such a multiverse, Robin Collins, among others, has noted that the universe-generator version, currently the most fashionable of the multiverse explanation, does not really explain how our universe came to be fine-tuned at all but only kicks the problem of explanation one step back. This is because the multiverse generator itself would require mechanisms to produce not only the massive variety of universes, but also at least one that is life-sustaining, namely, ours and thus would require an explanation for who or what created and designed the universe generator.[34] Indeed, Collins goes further and speculates that when some scientists talk about the multiverse, it is actually their way of doing metaphysics without using the "G" word.[35]

So how can we explain a phenomenon like fine-tuning? Paul Davies, a British astrophysicist and professor at Arizona State University, puts it this way:

> There is for me powerful evidence that there is something going on behind it all. . . . It seems as though somebody has fine-tuned nature's numbers to make the Universe. . . . The impression of design is overwhelming.[36]

Davies is asserting here that the existence of a fine-tuned universe, something widely agreed-upon in the scientific community, is a sign pointing to a cosmic designer. Interestingly, Professor Susskind admits up front that a creator God behind the universe would explain fine-tuning as well, but, as an atheist, this is not a solution he prefers. Whether he, or anyone else, can be satisfied with another explanation for the fine-tuning, such as chance or

34. Closer to Truth, "Did God Create Multiple Universes?"
35. Collins's reference in Craig, "Has the Multiverse Replaced God?"
36. Davies, *Cosmic Blueprint*, 203.

a multiverse, is something each reader will need to contemplate. Either way, the sign of fine-tuning remains to be considered with care.

Counterargument

One objection often brought against arguments for God based upon observed design in the universe is articulated by American atheist and writer George H. Smith. Any argument for God from design, he says,

> Assumes that if life needs explaining, the positing of a god provides that explanation. But this, of course, explains nothing. If god himself is in any sense alive, then he must also be the result of conscious design by a supergod—and so on into our familiar regress.[37]

Smith's point is that God fails as an explanation for life on earth for the simple reason that God too is alive. In other words, God exhibits some of the same characteristics for which a designer is allegedly needed so he too requires a designer to explain his life. Smith goes further and states that if life needs to be caused, then God's life too needs to be caused by some other being (a supergod), and that by another, and so on, leading to an infinite regress of causes. In other words, we have solved nothing by arguing that life requires an explanation and putting forward God as the being who could create it. We have simply ended up in an infinite regress of causes.

What are we to say to this objection? Contrary to Smith's understanding, the argument does not assert that *every instance* of life needs to be caused or explained, only *life which is created, which came into being*. This is a vital difference and should be remembered by those who use this argument. Nor is it one Christians have simply come up with to answer challenges like this. It is part of long-standing Christian theology. Furthermore, it is actually a rather obvious point when we remember that in order to be caused

37. Smith, *Atheism*, 269.

or created, an entity must, at some point, come into being. If a living person or thing turns out to be eternal, having no beginning or end, then that entity never came into being. It always was and, therefore, not only would not *need* to be caused by another, but it *could not* have been caused by anything. It would be an instance of a living being which needs no further explanation.

God, by definition, is precisely this kind of being. He is an eternal beginningless being and, therefore, one who needs no cause or further explanation since he always was. We see this portrayal of God in the biblical record itself, where God identified himself as the "I am" in two places (Exod 3:14; John 8:58). In other words, God is the being that just is. He received his own existence from no other cause. As an eternal being with no beginning or end, he can explain the existence of life on earth while he himself needs no further explanation.

SIGN SIX: THE EXISTENCE OF OUR UNIVERSE POINTS TO GOD

Earlier we noted that certain features of our universe, including its fine-tuning, the existence of DNA, and the presence of minds in the universe, point to a creator. But what about the very existence of the universe itself? Could the simple fact that the universe exists be one more sign pointing to a creator?

There is good reason for thinking so, and it starts with an application of a well-known maxim referred to earlier in this book: *ex nihilo, nihil fit*, "out of nothing, nothing comes." This principle asserts something which is hard to deny, namely, that if something, whether it be a baseball bat, coffee cup, spaceship, or universe, comes into being, then it must have been brought into being by a cause sufficient for the task. Everything which began to exist requires a cause. Applied to our universe, it indicates that since our universe came into existence, it, too, must have a cause and one that is sufficient to produce a universe.

This principle is widely accepted in philosophy, science, and in all of life generally. It is nothing more than a recognition of the obvious idea that things do not pop into existence out of nothing. If something begins to exist, it must have a cause.

This principle has been a key element in both philosophical and scientific arguments about the origin of our universe. One such philosophical argument has been advanced by American philosopher J. P. Moreland but goes back as far as the ancient Greek philosopher Aristotle, who lived from 384 to 322 BCE. We will turn to it first.

A Philosophical Analysis

The key claim in this philosophical argument can be stated as follows: The fact that things exist now means something always existed. This is based upon a rigorous application of the maxim mentioned above—*ex nihilo, nihil fit*, out of nothing, nothing comes. It means that the simple fact that things exist today all around us means that something must *always have existed* in the past. In other words, there never was a time when *nothing* existed. There could not have been such a time, otherwise there would be nothing now.

This leads to an interesting question, however, namely, if there was something existing when we go back far enough, what kind of being, or beings, were back there? Two choices are normally suggested. The first is that there could be an infinite regress of dependent entities, each being caused by something before it, with the process going back forever with no beginning. Second, there could be a first uncaused cause which gave existence to all other things.

While some are drawn to the idea of an infinite regress, it has always faced the question that if everything that exists received existence from something before it, then how did the entire series of dependent caused beings come into being at all? In other words, if all you have in your explanation of the existence of things is a series of entities, *all of which had to be caused* by something before them, then how did this entire series of existing things come into being? How did anything come to exist at all?[38]

Philosopher J. P. Moreland offers the following interesting story to illustrate this question. Imagine your friend asks if he can borrow your iPad. You reply, "I'd be happy to lend you one if I had one, but I don't. But no problem, let me borrow one from a friend and pass it on to you." Alas, when you ask your friend for one, he replies that he just sold his but will try to borrow one from a different friend and pass it on to you. Suppose this friend asks yet a different person and receives the same response and imagine this process keeps on going and going with no one ever being found who has an iPad to lend.

Two questions arise at this point. First, will your friend ever get an iPad? The answer seems patently obvious. No, he will not. How could he? Second, suppose we see him a week later *with an iPad* under his arm? What does that tell us? Easy. It reveals that, after a few rounds of asking, someone up the chain was found who owned an iPad, someone who did not need to borrow one from a friend. This person then lent it, and eventually it got passed along to your friend.[39]

How does this relate to our earlier question about the existence of all things? Moreland asks us to substitute *existence* in place of the iPad and then run through the same mental exercise. Once you accept the principle that things do not pop into existence by themselves, it follows that if something exists, it must have received that existence from something outside itself. Things that exist must be caused by something before them. And here is Moreland's point: If all we have to explain the existence of things is prior causes, which themselves had to receive existence from something before them, and these causes had to receive their existence from something prior, and so on forever with no being ever having existence on its own to give to others, then how did anything come to exist at all? Just like seeing our friend with the iPad, when we see things existing today, it means that somewhere up the chain, a being was

38. Clarke, *Demonstration of the Being*, 5–8.

39. Moreland, "Arguments for the Existence of God."

found which had existence *which it did not need to receive from something else*, which it could then pass on to others.

To put it straightforwardly, the fact that you and I exist today means that some being up the chain had existence *on its own* which it did not need to acquire from something else. As Aristotle put it, there must be an unmoved mover or, we might say, an uncaused cause.[40] As the great Aristotelian Christian theologian and philosopher Thomas Aquinas put it, this is the being we call God.[41]

As noted in the previous chapter, this fits with the Bible's own description of God. He identified himself as the "I am" in two places (Exod 3:14; John 8:58). In other words, God is the being that just is. He received his own existence from no other being. In this way, he perfectly explains how the entire series of existing things received their existence.

As noted above, there is another way of approaching this question, a scientific one. Many scientists also ask the question we are asking here, namely, how our universe come to be, and to their answers we turn now.

Two Scientific Analyses

Big Bang Cosmology

Did our universe have a beginning? As most of us probably know, the current widely accepted cosmology is called Big Bang Cosmology and is accepted by most scientists, theists and atheists alike. This, of course, does not automatically guarantee it is correct, but it does show that the evidence for it is deemed to be strong enough by scientists of all stripes that most have embraced it.

The fundamental assertion of Big Bang Cosmology is that a finite time ago our universe was shrunk down to a point sometimes referred to as infinite density from which it expanded at a high rate and became the universe it is today. The term "infinite

40. Aristotle, *Metaphysics* 12.1072a.

41. Aquinas, *Summa Theologiae* Ia.1 and Ia.2.3. See also Aquinas, *Summa Contra Gentiles* 1.13.28:94.

density" is an interesting one because, when we think about it, no actual object could truly possess infinite density. Any object that had any size at all, no matter how small, could be still smaller. It could be cut in half and then cut in half again and again and . . . well, you get the picture. This means that if a being truly is infinitely dense, then it is equivalent to nothing, which is why the big bang is often referred to as an event in which our universe came into being out of nothing. While there is some debate about *when* this astounding event occurred and what it means, there is little debate that it *did* happen.

Science journalist Matt Williams, writing in *Universe Today*, describes the big bang theory this way:

> In short, the Big Bang hypothesis states that all of the current and past matter in the Universe came into existence at the same time. . . . At this time, all matter was compacted into a very small ball with infinite density and intense heat called a Singularity. Suddenly, the Singularity began expanding, and the universe as we know it began.[42]

Physicists and cosmologists John D. Barrow and Frank J. Tipler describe it in these words:

> At this singularity, space and time came into existence; literally nothing existed before the singularity, so, if the Universe originated at such a singularity, we would truly have a creation *ex nihilo*.[43]

It is a fascinating concept, and much of our knowledge of it stems from a discovery made by Edwin Hubble, after whom the famous Hubble telescope is named. Hubble was an American astronomer who lived from 1889 to 1953. In 1929, he was peering through his powerful telescope far into the distance and began to notice something that has now become widely accepted but was unknown at the time. The planets and stars were moving further apart from each other while the relationship between them was

42. Williams, "Big Bang Theory."

43. Barrow and Tipler, *Anthropic Cosmological Principle*, 442.

remaining constant, much like a balloon with polka dots on it being blown up. He, and other members of the scientific community, immediately realized the implications of this finding were dramatic. Over time, it was seen that if one could wind the tape backwards, the universe would be getting smaller and smaller, eventually reaching a point of singularity referred to in the quotations above, from which the entire process of expansion began.

J. Richard Gott, professor of astrophysical sciences at Princeton University and known for his work on such interesting topics as time travel, explains the significance of Hubble's discovery in these words:

> The upshot of Hubble's discovery was that at some point in the finite past—probably around 15 billion years ago—the entire known universe was contracted down to a single mathematical point which marked the origin of the universe. That initial explosion has come to be known as the "Big Bang." . . . The universe began from a state of infinite density. . . . Space and time were created in that event and so was all the matter in the universe. It is not meaningful to ask what happened before the Big Bang; it is like asking what is north of the North Pole. Similarly, it is not sensible to ask where the Big Bang took place. The point-universe was not an object isolated in space; it was the entire universe, and so the answer can only be that the Big Bang happened everywhere.[44]

This event marked the beginning of our universe and is especially remarkable when one considers the fact that a state of infinite density is synonymous with nothing. It means the universe had a beginning; it came into existence, and thus needs a cause.

There is another, completely different, type of scientific analysis which also points to the universe having a beginning and thus needing a cause.

44. Gott, "Will the Universe Expand?," 65.

The Laws of Thermodynamics

The idea that our universe had a beginning and is not eternal is also indicated by the second law of thermodynamics, which is about as close as we can get to an iron clad law of science. It is widely accepted across the scientific community and is one of the four laws of thermodynamics. The first is that energy can neither be created nor destroyed. The total amount of energy in the universe stays the same over time. The second law concerns the nature of this energy and states that as energy is used and transformed, more of it becomes evenly distributed throughout the universe and, thus, unavailable to do the work of the universe.[45]

To see how this works, think of how you might react if you walked into an empty room early in the morning, switched on the lights believing you were the first one there that day and, to your surprise, found a hot cup of coffee sitting on a nearby table. It would suddenly dawn on you that someone else had arrived there before you. Why the lights were out, the door locked, and no one was in sight might confound you, but you would know someone had been in the room recently. Otherwise, the coffee would be cold.

The same would be true for someone entering a bathroom and finding the tub full of hot water. It would be even more startling to find the bathtub with warm water at one end and cool water at the other. We would know someone had been there recently and added hot water to the tub. Our experience has told us that heat from the coffee, if left in a room overnight, will eventually become evenly distributed throughout the room. It also tells us that the hot water poured into one end of the bathtub will soon become evenly distributed throughout the rest of the tub, and it will all become the same temperature. Once this happens, that energy is no longer available to heat the coffee or the water in the front of the bathtub. We would need a new supply of energy for that.

When we apply the second law of thermodynamics to the universe as a whole, it means that, over time, the energy of the

45. Lucas and Hamer, "Second Law of Thermodynamics."

universe is being evenly distributed throughout the universe. The effect is that the energy available to do the work of our universe is running down, and the universe is moving toward a disordered state, sometimes called entropy. Our universe can be compared to a locomotive moving down the track, burning fuel from its tanks as it goes. There are two things we know about this locomotive. First, it has not been chugging down the track forever, otherwise it would have run out of fuel a long time ago. Second, it will not be moving down the track forever. At some point it will run out of fuel.

The same two inferences follow from the second law of thermodynamics for our universe as a whole. First, it, too, will not go on forever. It will all come to an end one day because the energy available to do the work of the universe will run out. It will reach a state of entropy, sometimes called the heat death of the universe. Second, and more importantly for our purposes, it means the universe has not been operating forever, otherwise the energy would have been used up already. It had a beginning in the initial event called the big bang. At a certain point in the finite past, it came into existence, from a point of infinite density. It thus needs a cause. *Ex nihilo, nihil fit*. Out of nothing, nothing comes.

Atheist philosopher Kai Nielsen, who was mentioned earlier in this book acknowledging that atheists need to provide reasons for their view just as theists do, has also contended that things do not come from nothing. Recall his invitation to his audience to consider how they would react if they heard a loud bang in the lobby of the auditorium behind them, only to be told that nothing caused the bang; it just sounded off all on its own. They would not accept that explanation, he said. In fact, he added, they would see it as "quite unintelligible."[46]

Nielsen was right, of course, and it is not a stretch to say that this same principle applies to big bangs too. Furthermore, just as the cause of Nielsen's loud bang in the back of the auditorium

46. This illustration was used in a public debate between Kai Nielsen and Christian philosopher William Lane Craig on the topic of "God, Morality, and Evil" at the University of Western Ontario, February, 1991.

would need to be something capable of producing such a sound, the cause of the universe would need to be supernatural (outside of the universe which it caused) and immensely powerful, capable of producing a universe like ours.

It will come as no surprise that the contention that the big bang requires a creator—God—to explain it does not sit well with everyone. American philosopher and well-known atheist Quentin Smith, writing in *Faith and Philosophy*, argued that we are not actually warranted in claiming that the singularity referred to by the scientists above, namely the big bang, is equivalent to nothing simply because it has zero volume and zero duration. He contended that cosmologists are able to think of an entity that has zero dimensions, like a spatial point, as being real. In other words, it is not clear, he argued, that the big bang really represents the universe coming into existence from nothing, and therefore needing a cause like God.[47]

The question Smith is raising concerns the actual meaning of *nothing* in this situation. Does nothing really mean "nothing," or does it mean "something"? Here is where the term "infinite density" mentioned above becomes important because, as noted earlier, no real object, no "something," could actually possess infinite density since if it had any size at all, no matter how small, it could be still smaller. It could be split in half and then split in half again and again.

It's why the Cambridge University astronomer Fred Hoyle has come right out and stated that Big Bang Cosmology requires "the creation of matter from nothing." If we go back far enough, he says, the universe was "shrunk down to nothing at all."[48] In his mind, nothing means nothing. If so, it requires a cause sufficient to produce it. *Ex nihilo, nihil fit.*

47. Smith, "Big Bang Cosmological Argument," 226–27.

48. Hoyle, *From Stonehenge to Modern Cosmology*, 36.

Counterargument

One response commonly given to arguments pointing to the existence of the universe as evidence for God is that if everything that exists requires a cause, then God, too, would require a cause. But then, that cause would require another cause, and so on leading to an infinite regress of causes. This means that we have solved nothing by positing a supernatural cause of the universe. We have merely pushed the question of causation back one step, and now the question becomes, "What caused God?"

This objection is reminiscent of one articulated earlier by the atheist writer George H. Smith against the argument from *design*. Smith also raises this new objection against the argument for God based on the *existence* of the universe. Notice precisely how he frames the argument before raising his main question concerning it. In his words, this argument begins by stating that "every existing thing has a cause, and every cause must be caused by a prior cause."[49] A few pages later, he raises the question, "If everything has a cause, how did God become exempt?"[50]

Smith's point is that if everything requires a cause, then God, too, if there is one, would require a cause and this would lead to an infinite regress of causes. Not much of a solution, he thinks.

Do Smith, and others who argue this way, have a point? He would indeed if this argument stated that *everything that exists* requires a cause, as Smith clearly thinks, but it does not. If you have been reading carefully, you will know that this is not how the argument was stated above. Rather, it stated that everything *that began to exist* requires a cause. This is an important difference and, unfortunately, one that is sometimes missed by both Christians and non-Christians alike in the way they state this argument.

It is important to note that the Latin maxim referred to above—*ex nihilo, nihil fit* ("out of nothing, nothing comes")—does not state that absolutely everything in existence requires a cause, only that things which *came into being* require causes. And that is

49. Smith, *Atheism*, 236.

50. Smith, *Atheism*, 239.

precisely what this argument states, i.e., everything which came into being at some point requires a cause. Since everything in our experience came into being and thus require causes, it is natural for us to fall into the assumption that absolutely everything that exists requires a cause. A moment's reflection, however, reveals that it would not include God since he, by definition, is an eternal being with no beginning or end. A being like this would not *need* a cause but it *could not have one* since the being always was. The answer to the question—What caused God?—is actually quite straightforward. Nothing caused God since God always was. God never came into being and therefore could have no cause.

It may be worth reminding ourselves of something said earlier, namely, that not only is God, by definition, an eternal beginningless being who needs no cause or further explanation since he always was, but also that this fits the description of God presented to us in the Bible. In two places God identified himself as the "I am," a being that just is (Exod 3:14; John 8:58). He received his own existence from no other cause. As an eternal being with no beginning or end, he can explain the existence of life on earth while he, himself, needs no further explanation.

Conclusion

WHY THIS MATTERS FOR OUR CONVERSATIONS

A FRIEND OF MINE named Dan is a thoughtful and informed Christian. He is formally trained in theology and philosophy, but his vocation is music. As a longtime member of a successful band, he has performed widely in many different venues. As such, his world is filled with people who know little about faith or religion and often care for it even less. When they hear about Dan's vibrant faith, as they will sooner or later, most are surprised. It's not what they were expecting. It's not uncommon for someone to approach Dan and tell him outright that they think his belief in God is simply irrational. That's the term—"irrational." How might you respond if someone labelled your faith that way?

Dan is not willing to let that statement stand. As he has told me numerous times, "We are called to be nice, but not timid." His response is usually something like this: "Actually, I think belief in God is a more rational view than atheism." Now that he has their attention, he continues, "Atheism has some heavy lifting to do to explain the existence of some important things in our world like the world itself, minds and consciousness, real morality, love, beauty, and a few other things. On the other hand," he continues, "if there is an eternal Mind behind it all, all of these things make sense and are quite easy to explain. In the absence of this eternal mind, atheism is left having to say that the universe and all these other things sprung into existence with no cause. That doesn't sound like the more rational view to me."

I appreciate Dan and others like him. They are not keeping their heads down and going through life hoping no one will raise the topic of religion. On the contrary, they are willing to engage others on the merits of Christian theism and point out that it has explanatory power which is unnoticed by many. It can account for a number of highly significant realities in our world, such as the ones mentioned above, in a way that atheism cannot. We should all heed Dan's advice that we are called to be nice but not timid, especially when the stakes are as high as they are in a discussion concerning what stands behind our world. My hat is off to people like Dan!

Bibliography

Aquinas, Thomas. *Summa Contra Gentiles*. Notre Dame, IN: University of Notre Dame Press, 1975.

———. *Summa Theologiae*. Translated by Fathers of the English Dominican. Christian Classics. https://www.ccel.org/a/aquinas/summa/home.html.

Aristotle. *Metaphysics*. In *The Complete Works of Aristotle: The Revised Oxford Translation*, edited by Jonathan Barnes, 2:1552–1728. Princeton: Princeton University Press, 1984.

Ashmore, Robert. *Building a Moral System*. Englewood Cliffs, NJ: Prentice Hall, 1987.

Ayer, A. J. *Language, Truth, and Logic*. London: Gollancz, 1936.

Barrow, John D., and Frank J. Tipler. *The Anthropic Cosmological Principle*. Rev. ed. Oxford: Oxford University Press, 1988.

Beauchamp, Tom L. *Philosophical Ethics: An Introduction to Moral Philosophy*. New York: McGraw-Hill, 1982.

Beckwith, Francis J. "A Critique of Moral Relativism." In *Do the Right Thing: Readings in Applied Ethics and Social Philosophy*, edited by Francis J. Beckwith, 12–21. Belmont, CA: Wadsworth, 2002.

Benedict, Ruth. "A Defense of Moral Relativism." In *Do the Right Thing: Readings in Applied Ethics and Social Philosophy*, edited by Francis J. Beckwith, 6–11. Belmont, CA: Wadsworth, 2002.

———. *Patterns of Culture*. Boston: Houghton & Mifflin, 1989.

Biola University. "Does God Exist? William Lane Craig vs. Christopher Hitchens—Full Debate." *YouTube*, Sept. 28, 2014. https://www.youtube.com/watch?v=0tYm41hb48o&t=3604s.

Bullivant, Stephen. "Defining 'Atheism.'" In *The Oxford Handbook of Atheism*, edited by Stephen Bullivant and Michael Ruse, 11–21. New York: Oxford University Press, 2013.

Bullivant, Stephen, and Michael Ruse, eds. *The Oxford Handbook of Atheism*. New York: Oxford University Press, 2013.

Carrier, Richard C. *Why I Am Not a Christian: Four Conclusive Reasons to Reject the Faith*. Richmond, CA: Philosophy, 2011.

Chamberlain, Paul. *Why People Don't Believe: Confronting Seven Challenges to Christian Faith*. Grand Rapids: Baker, 2011.

Clarke, Samuel. *A Demonstration of the Being and Attributes of God More Particularly in Answer to Hobbes, Spinoza, and Their Followers.* https://www.earlymoderntexts.com/assets/pdfs/clarke1704.pdf.

Closer to Truth. "Did God Create Multiple Universes?" *YouTube*, Mar. 20, 2017. https://www.youtube.com/watch?v=MVlNItEoRw4.

———. "Leonard Susskind: Is the Universe Fine-Tuned for Life and Mind?" *YouTube*, Jan. 8, 2013. https://www.youtube.com/watch?v=2cT4zZIHR3s.

Collins, Francis S. *The Language of God: A Scientist Presents Evidence for Belief.* New York: Free Press, 2006.

Craig, William Lane. "Has the Multiverse Replaced God?" *Reasonable Faith.* https://www.reasonablefaith.org/writings/popular-writings/existence-nature-of-god/has-the-multiverse-replaced-god.

Davies, Paul. *The Cosmic Blueprint: New Discoveries in Nature's Creative Ability to Order the Universe.* New York: Simon and Schuster, 1988.

Dawkins, Richard. *The God Delusion.* Boston: Houghton Mifflin, 2006.

Dennett, Daniel C. *Breaking the Spell: Religion as a Natural Phenomenon.* New York: Penguin, 2006.

Drcraigvideos. "Atheism Redefined as Absence of Belief." *YouTube*, Apr. 26, 2011. https://www.youtube.com/watch?v=XcuSMQVq5dM&t=1s.

———. "The Great Easter Debate: William Lane Craig vs. Brian Edwards." *YouTube*, Apr. 16, 2011. https://www.youtube.com/watch?v=W6MRMp9yoro.

Gambetta, Diego., ed. *Making Sense of Suicide Missions.* Oxford: Oxford University Press, 2005.

Geisler, Norman L., and Winfried Corduan. *Philosophy of Religion.* 2nd ed. Grand Rapids: Baker, 1988.

Goldbert, Sanford C., ed. *The Brain in a Vat.* Cambridge: Cambridge University Press, 2016.

Gott, J. Richard. "Will the Universe Expand Forever?" *Scientific American* 234 (1976) 62–79.

Haldane, J. B. S. *Possible Worlds and Other Essays.* London: Chatto and Windus, 1927.

Harris, Sam. *The End of Faith: Religion, Terror, and the Future of Reason.* New York: Norton, 2005.

Hoyle, Fred. *From Stonehenge to Modern Cosmology.* San Francisco: Freeman, 1972.

Jillette, Penn. *God? No! Signs You May Already Be an Atheist and Other Magical Tales.* New York: Simon & Schuster, 2011.

Kain, Erik. "Penn Jillette on Atheism and Libertarianism." *Forbes*, Aug. 17, 2011. https://www.forbes.com/sites/erikkain/2011/08/17/penn-jillette-on-atheism-and-libertarianism/.

Lennox, John C. *God and Stephen Hawking: Whose Design Is it Anyway?* Oxford: Lion, 2011.

———. *God's Undertaker: Has Science Buried God?* Oxford: Lion, 2009.

Lewis, C. S. *The Abolition of Man.* New York: Macmillan, 1955.

———. *Mere Christianity*. New York: Touchstone, 1980.
———. *Miracles*. San Francisco: HarperCollins, 1947.
———. *The Problem of Pain*. New York: Macmillan, 1962.
———. "Religion Without Dogma?" In *C. S. Lewis Essay Collection: Faith, Christianity, and the Church*, edited by Lesley Walmsley, 163–79. London: HarperCollins, 2002.
———. *Surprised by Joy: The Shape of My Early Life*. London: Bles, 1955.
Loftus, John. *Why I Became an Atheist: A Former Preacher Rejects Christianity*. Amherst, NY: Prometheus, 2008.
Lucas, Jim, and Ashley Hamer. "What Is the Second Law of Thermodynamics?" *Livescience*, Feb. 7, 2022. https://www.livescience.com/50941-second-law-thermodynamics.html.
Marshall, Paul, ed. *Religious Freedom in the World*. Lanham, MD: Rowman & Littlefield, 2008.
———. *Their Blood Cries Out: The Worldwide Tragedy of Modern Christians Who Are Dying for Their Faith*. Nashville: Word, 1997.
McGrath, Alister, and Joanna Collicutt McGrath. *The Dawkins Delusion: Atheist Fundamentalism and the Denial of the Divine*. Downers Grove, IL: InterVarsity, 2007.
Moreland, J. P. "Arguments for the Existence of God." *YouTube*, Mar. 11, 2015. https://www.youtube.com/watch?v=TkrJLbiY5hY.
———. *Scaling the Secular City*. Grand Rapids: Baker, 1987.
Naga Seminarian. "John Lennox Wisely Responds to a Confused Atheist on 'Does Morality Exist Without God?'" *YouTube*, Apr. 23, 2025. https://www.youtube.com/watch?v=i8uKFQ-7TqE.
Nagel, Thomas. *Mind and Cosmos*. Oxford: Oxford University Press, 2012.
Navabi, Armin. *Why There Is No God: Simple Responses to 20 Common Arguments for the Existence of God*. Edited by Nicki Hise. CreateSpace, 2014.
Nielsen, Kai. *Reason and Practice: A Modern Introduction to Philosophy*. New York: Harper&Row, 1971.
Open Doors. "Christians Found Killed in Church in DRC." Feb. 25, 2025. https://www.opendoorsuk.org/news/latest-news/drc-attack-church/.
———. "World Watch List 2025." https://www.opendoors.org/en-US/persecution/countries/.
Oppy, Graham. "Arguments for Atheism." In *The Oxford Handbook of Atheism*, edited by Stephen Bullivant and Michael Ruse, 53–70. New York: Oxford University Press, 2013.
Pape, Robert A. *Dying to Win: The Strategic Logic of Suicide Terrorism*. New York: Random House, 2005.
Persecution.org. "Write Letters to Prisoners of Faith." https://www.persecution.org/letters/.
Plantinga, Alvin. *God, Freedom, and Evil*. Grand Rapids: Eerdmans, 1977.
———. *Warranted Christian Belief*. New York: Oxford University Press, 2000.

———. *Where the Conflict Really Lies: Science, Religion, and Naturalism*. Oxford: Oxford University Press, 2011.

The Preachers. "Penn Jillette Explains His Atheism to the Preachers." *YouTube*, July 19, 2016. https://www.youtube.com/watch?v=oKGjHmeKUQs.

Rachels, James. "A Critique of Ethical Relativism." In *Philosophy: The Quest for Truth*, edited by Louis P. Pojman, 317–25. Belmont, CA: Wadsworth, 1989.

Reasonable Faith. "Atheism Shmatheism." *Facebook*, July 24, 2018. https://www.facebook.com/watch/?v=10155947998913229.

Russell, Bertrand. *The Basic Writings of Bertrand Russell*. Edited by Robert E. Egner and Lester E. Denon. New York: Routledge, 2009.

Savage, C. Wade. "The Paradox of the Stone." *Philosophical Review* 76 (1967) 74–79.

Smith, George H. *Atheism: The Case Against God*. Amherst, NY: Prometheus, 2016.

Smith, Quentin. "A Big Bang Cosmological Argument for God's Nonexistence." *Faith and Philosophy* 9 (1992) 217–37.

Templeton Prize. "Evolutionary Argument Against Naturalism." *YouTube*, Apr. 25, 2017. https://www.youtube.com/watch?v=cs6zFymVKJM&t=578s.

Theworldvideos1. "Richard Dawkins: 'God Is the Same as Fairies.'" *YouTube*, Feb. 5, 2010. https://www.youtube.com/watch?v=CQcJ_y33Luo.

Tilley, John J. "Cultural Relativism." *Human Rights Quarterly* 22 (2000) 501–47.

UNIFO Staff, ed. *International Human Rights Instruments of the United Nations, 1948–1982*. Pleasantville, NY: UNIFO, 1983.

Walmsley, Lesley, ed. *C. S. Lewis Essay Collection: Faith, Christianity and the Church*. London: HarperCollins, 2002.

Williams, Matt. "Big Bang Theory." *Universe Today*, Dec. 17, 2015. https://www.universetoday.com/articles/what-is-the-big-bang-theory.

Wolff, Jonathan. *An Introduction to Moral Philosophy*. New York: Norton, 2018.

www.ingramcontent.com/pod-product-compliance
Lightning Source LLC
LaVergne TN
LVHW090524110826
845146LV00003B/976

* 9 7 9 8 3 8 5 2 1 8 8 3 7 *